PRAISE FOR *TURNING LIFE INTO FICTION* FROM TEACHERS OF CREATIVE WRITING

What I like best about Robin Hemley's approach is that he engages the reader as an artist, as someone attempting something inherently important and worthy. I like the tone, too. The enthusiasm he shows for the craft is so tangible that you feel caught in a remarkable dialogue with an energetic and original teacher, who draws you into his life by revealing it through stories, and who encourages you to do the same for your readers.

—*Tom Chiarella*
DePauw University

As readers, we enter stories to learn how to read our lives; as writers, we search our lives for the hidden stories. When we are guided in these processes by a writer and teacher as generous as Robin Hemley, we are twice blessed. *Turning Life Into Fiction* may not make our lives storybook perfect, but it will help us mine the small gems embedded there.

—*Rebecca McClanahan*
University of North Carolina—Charlotte

Robin Hemley has managed to organize into a cohesive, entertaining and illuminating book, the terrifying chaos that confronts all fiction writers. Addressing ethical questions as well as technical ones, Hemley has created a blueprint for both the fiction writing instructor and the student. His generosity and enthusiasm remind us that, in our traumatic and often thankless struggle with the written word, we are not alone.

—*Kaylie Jones*
Southampton College

I found *Turning Life Into Fiction* helpful for teaching students how to *think* about writing. So much of what Hemley talks about is his own writing process. He examines it in useful ways.

—*Julie Barak*
Virginia Commonwealth University

At the same time lighthearted and entertaining, *Turning Life Into Fiction* is a practical text for my fiction writing class. Hemley expertly addresses a problem most beginning fiction writers have—how to turn personal experiences into the basis for solid fiction.

—*Sheila Schwartz*
Cleveland State

Hemley's *Turning Life Into Fiction* is the first textbook I've used in my writing classes that my students truly enjoyed. They found his anecdotes, explanations, and exercises readable and practical. I, too, find his prose insightful and clear. The book is a joy to use.

—*Karen Shoemaker*
University of Nebraska—Lincoln

A very helpful book. *Turning Life Into Fiction* teaches the techniques necessary for beginning writers to gather their personal experiences and then, using the ingenious exercises designed to help them distance themselves from these experiences, change and restructure them into fiction.

—*Diane McPherson*
Ithaca College

This book gives the students a sense of having two teachers for the price of one: the one who stands before them, guiding them through a discussion of their own work in progress, the other who speaks to them through the pages of *Turning Life Into Fiction*, charming them with exemplary stories and insightful comments into the process of composing a story.

—*Richard Chess*
University of North Carolina—Asheville

Turning Life Into Fiction gives my students the confidence to work with material from their own lives, which is important for developing that all-elusive thing we call "voice." Their efforts were stronger and more interesting, especially in terms of structure and scene development. Robin Hemley gets them thinking about themselves as people who have something worth writing about.

—*Geeta N. Kothari*
University of Pittsburgh

TURNING LIFE
INTO FICTION

ROBIN HEMLEY

STORY PRESS
CINCINNATI, OHIO

01 00 99 98 97   5 4 3 2 1

Library of Congress Cataloging-in-Publication Data

Hemley, Robin
  Turning life into fiction / Robin Hemley.
      p.   cm.
  Includes index.
  ISBN 1-884910-37-8
  1. Fiction—Authorship—Problems, exercises, etc. 2. Autobiography—
  Authorship—Problems, exercises, etc. I. Title.
PN3355.H45   1994
808.3—dc20   94-18986
                                                                  CIP

Designed by Clare Finney

The permissions on the following page constitute an extension of this copyright page.

ABOUT THE AUTHOR

Robin Hemley has published two collections of short stories, *All You Can Eat* (Atlantic Monthly Press) and *The Big Ear* (John F. Blair), as well as a novel, *The Last Studebaker* (Graywolf Press). His stories have been anthologized in *Pushcart Prize XV* and in *Twenty Under Thirty* (Scribner's). He has won two PEN/Syndicated Fiction Awards, the Hugh J. Luke Award from *Prairie Schooner*, the George Garrett Award from *Willow Springs*, the Word Beat Press Award and the Walter Rumsey Marvin Award from the Ohioanna Library Association. He teaches fiction and creative nonfiction writing at Western Washington University in Bellingham, Washington.

For my teacher, Barry Hannah

ACKNOWLEDGMENTS

I want to thank the following people
for their help in the writing of this book:

Charles Baxter

Madison Smartt Bell

Philip Gerard

Judy Goldman

Jack Heffron

David Michael Kaplan

Nanci Kincaid

Bret Lott

Josip Novakovich

David Rosenthal

Lois Rosenthal

Jerry Saviano

David Shields

Sharon Solwitz

Peter Turchi

Steve Yarbrough

I'm also grateful to the
University of North Carolina at Charlotte.

Contents

Experience Versus the Imagination: A Transformation

W hat kind of fiction do you write?" I've been asked more than once.

"What do you mean?" I ask.

"Do you write true fiction?" I'm asked.

This question always stumps me. I stammer in bewilderment for a bit and come up with some unsatisfactory answer about how I sometimes write from my experiences. But that makes me sound like I'm a writer of true confessions.

I don't mind when people ask me if anything in my stories is autobiographical. For me, the two questions are different. The people who want to know if I write true fiction make me bristle. I think the trouble lies in that true things (things that really happened in real life to someone really real) are sometimes considered more important than things that never happened. On the other hand, people sometimes want to know what really happened because they're interested in the process of changing experience into fiction. I don't think there's anything wrong with that.

Someone once told me she didn't believe in autobiographical fiction, that if it wasn't completely imagined, one wasn't writing fiction. That's such an absurd statement I'm sure I'll remember it my whole life. Good fiction depends on the perceptions and observations of the writer, not on the source of the material.

Still, many writers distrust fiction that smacks of autobiography. They believe that autobiographical fiction represents in some way a failure of the writer's imagination, or that such writers have only "one good book" in them and, after they have finished their autobiographical effort, they will have spent their creativity and no more will be heard from them. There's an air of smugness in that kind of attitude. The writer who makes such a claim is, in effect, saying, first, "Autobiographical writing is not *real* writing," and second, "I'm a real writer, and people who want to be real writers should write like me — that is, from the unlimited stores of my superior imagination!"

Such a writer might point to Harper Lee's semi-autobiographical book, *To Kill a Mockingbird*, as an example of the pitfalls of autobiographical writing. Until a couple of years ago, I wasn't sure if Lee was still alive, so I went to the library and found that she was supposedly working on a second novel. That's a long time to wait for a second novel, but so what? If *To Kill a Mockingbird* is the one good book Harper will ever publish, that's not a fate worse than death. I'd settle for writing such a book.

There might be *some* truth in the fact that writers whose first novels are autobiographical find it more difficult than other writers to write a second novel, but writers of any stripe have a difficult time following a first novel. I've heard that as many as half of all first novelists never write a second.

There's definitely a tendency for writers to write autobiographical first novels — the standard coming-of-age novel, inevitably compared by one reviewer or another to *Catcher in the Rye* if the teenage protagonist is at all disaffected with society. And what teenager isn't? I'd bet that more reviewers use the protagonist Holden Caulfield as a comparison to the main character in the book they're reviewing than any other character, with perhaps the exception of Scout, the young protagonist of *To Kill a Mockingbird*. It's no wonder. Growing up is the natural territory of any young novelist, and there's absolutely nothing wrong with adding one's own version of this life transition to the pile. The overall experience of growing up might be the same for most people, but the individual details of each person's story are always unique, and that's what makes good fiction: the details.

For my part, I assiduously avoided writing a growing-up story for my first novel, *The Last Studebaker*. That, however, doesn't mean my novel was devoid of real-life experience. My novel is set in South Bend, Indiana, where I lived for a couple of years during high school, and where my mother still lives. Many of the details about South Bend in the book are things I have observed first-hand.

One of the main characters in the book, a woman named Lois, is loosely based on a friend with whom I used to frequent garage sales, which is one of the central activities of the book. My real-life friend has five children; the character in my book has two, neither of whom are much like any of my friend's children. The children in the book, an eleven-year-old girl named Meg and her sixteen-year-old sister, Gail, are modeled after myself, when I was Meg's age, and my brother Jonathan, who is five years older than me. The sexes are different but the behavior is much the same.

And that's the way it is throughout my novel. Plenty of incidents and characters are based on real life, but nearly all have been transformed. As we'll see in this book, transformation is the key to writing fiction based on real life.

Even the most autobiographical book stretches the truth from time to time, exaggerating and bending events to fit the story or the characters. And the most outlandish stories often contain some bit of real life or autobiography. The important fact to keep in mind is that a transformation is always involved. In writing fiction, a dialogue is always going on between one's personal experience and one's imagination.

Sometimes, I'll be discussing a story in a workshop, and several people will remark that a particular episode seems unbelievable.

"I just don't believe that Michael would stab Fran for saying that he had halitosis," one student will say.

"I agree completely," says another student.

The rest of the class nods.

At this point I look in the direction of the author and see that he has this smug look on his face, and I know what he's going to say next.

"But it really happened!" he says with an air of superiority, as though he's just pulled one over on us.

"It doesn't matter that it really happened," I explain as patiently as possible. "The question to ask is, 'Is it believable?' The worst defense a writer can use is the excuse, 'But it really happened!' "

The fact that something really happened does not make it good fiction. In fact, it's irrelevant, at least in terms of the story's quality. Plenty of things happen in real life that just don't seem believable on the page. On the other hand, the fact that it really happened shouldn't exclude the material from one's writing. The trick, of course, comes in molding the factual material to the specifications of one's fictional world.

With any kind of fiction, there are basically two ways to incorporate your real-life experiences. Either you write a story based on something that happened to you, or you write a largely imagined story, with snippets from your life woven into the basic fabric of the story. You might set your novel during the last ice age and your main characters might be a family of irritable mastodons. But the main mastodon, the way he chews his food with his mouth open, might clearly portray your father. In this way, every novel is based on real life. It's nearly impossible to stop our real lives from intruding into our fiction, even when the story is clearly not about ourselves.

We can even see real life bleeding into the fictional world of a writer as absurdist as Samuel Beckett. In a letter to a friend, he wrote of watching old men in the park flying kites "immense distances" and "right out of sight," and how transfixed he was by the sight. "My next old man or old young man [meaning his next character in a fictional work] must be a kite flier," he wrote. At the time, Beckett was working on his novel *Murphy* (Grove Press), and true to his word, he included the following scene in which an old man is lying in bed, imagining himself flying a kite. Note the similarities between the wording in his letter and that of the scene:

> "Before you go," said Mr. Kelly, "you might hand me the tail of my kite. Some tassels have come adrift."
>
> Celia went to the cupboard where he kept his kite, took out the tail and loose tassels and brought them over to the bed.
>
> "As you say," said Mr. Kelly, "hark to the wind. I shall fly her out of sight to-morrow."
>
> He fumbled vaguely at the coils of the tail. Already he was in position, straining his eyes for the speck that was he, digging in his heels against the immense pull skyward. Celia kissed him and left him.
>
> "God willing," said Mr. Kelly, "right out of sight."

I think that's a marvelous scene. You don't have to know anything about the book to feel the richness of this image of an old man lying in bed, pretending to fly his kite. Later in the book, Celia looks for Mr. Kelly in the park where other old men are flying their kites. Beckett has transformed his real-life experience in the way all good fiction writers do: building on the initial image, stretching it, exaggerating it, seeing how far he can take it.

In an interview with Robert S. Boone, novelist Ann Beattie claims she's "never written anything directly autobiographical. But at the same time I've never written anything that didn't honestly reflect some emotional state." She also says that she never directly transfers an overheard conversation into her fiction, but molds it to the story. "What I hear in a New York City restaurant will be cast in an Iowa City bus depot."

Let me tell you a couple of autobiographical stories.

One time in elementary school, I built a time machine in my art class. I announced that I was going to send Ann Holmes, a girl I had a crush on, back in time. My art teacher made a point of telling the class it wouldn't work. I insisted it would. Half the class believed my teacher, half believed me because, I suppose, I acted so confident in my invention, which was nothing more than a large cardboard box with Styrofoam knobs. The day came when the machine was ready. I helped Ann into the box, turned a few knobs and . . . Ann went back in time. Well, of course not. After a minute, Ann's voice, from inside the box, said, "I'm still here."

"No, you're not," I said.

Ann stepped out of the box and announced, "It didn't work."

"You see?" my teacher said.

"Good job, Bemel," said one of my classmates. Bemel was my nickname. Simply a strange bastardization of Hemley. It doesn't mean anything, but for some reason it still makes me cringe to think of it.

The teacher savored her victory and asked the class what lesson they had learned. Tony Trimball, a little turncoat who had just that morning asked to be the second person I sent back in time, raised his hand. He waved it around in that annoying, urgent manner of fourth grade boys.

"Yes, Tony?" the art teacher asked.

"Don't say things that aren't true."

Of course, I was ostracized for the rest of the day, and I didn't get many valentines that year. I was the fool, and it probably hurt me a lot at the time. Now I'm proud of my fourth grade self, just as I'm proud of other goofy things I did at that age, like wearing my pajamas to school because I bet my mother that I could get away with it. (A gentleman's bet, we used to call it; no money involved. My mom didn't encourage gambling.) I insisted that my pajamas looked like regular clothes. And I almost *did* get away with it. The only people who noticed were my fourth grade math teacher, Mrs. Hill, and her student assistant. During a math quiz, I noticed them looking my way and giggling. Mrs. Hill called me over to her desk and whispered, "Robin, are you wearing your pajamas?"

"No, Mrs. Hill."

"Are you sure?" she asked again, tilting her head slightly.

"Yes, Mrs. Hill."

I didn't like Mrs. Hill at the time, but now I do. She, too, could have humiliated me in front of the class, if she chose. She, unlike my art teacher, had an innate appreciation for the ridiculous, which, after all, isn't that far removed from the sublime. And you'd think the art teacher, not the math teacher, would be the one to foster my creativity.

I could say that these two stories about myself are untrue. Completely untrue. Didn't happen. Nada. No such person as Mrs. Hill. And my art teacher thought I was Picasso.

Would it matter that the stories didn't happen?

The question to ask is not, "Did it really happen?" but "Is it believable?" If it *could* have happened, if it has some relevance to what it means to be alive, that's all that matters. Believability. Authenticity. That's why "But it really happened!" is such a lame defense for a story you've written. If it doesn't seem believable, forget it. I'm not going to be moved by your story.

I do acknowledge there's such a thing as simple curiosity, so I'll tell you what's true and what's not true.

Both stories happened. Almost exactly as I told them. The key word is *almost*. The fictional part is in the details.

Mrs. Hill really was my fourth grade teacher and I really wore my pajamas to school, and that conversation occurred pretty much as I said it did. Of course, I couldn't vouch for every word. If I were writing a story about the pajama incident, I'd make up even more details to make the story seem believable. I'd tell you what the pajamas looked like. They must have been made out of some coarse material, not your typical satiny pj's, and the shirt probably had a collar.

And that whole thing with the art teacher happened as well. I'm pretty sure Ann Holmes was the one I sent back in time, though I'm not positive. It doesn't matter. It could have been Ann Holmes. The dialogue, of course, was made up, though something very similar was probably said.

Tony Trimball didn't exist, but Tony Turnbull did, and hopefully still does somewhere. Tony was my friend from first through sixth grade, when my family moved away.

My nickname was Bemel and it does give me a strange twinge when I recall the hated name. So in this case, I was being true to the emotional experience of being in fourth grade. It's a hundred times more important for the story to seem emotionally honest than for the story to be honest in the conventional sense.

I don't know if someone called me Bemel when the time machine failed. But when I came to that moment in the story, my mind just flashed, "Bemel." It's not only the details but the associations that count in writing fiction. All artists, not only fiction writers, have associative minds. One event recalls another. And part of fictionalizing material often involves putting two real details (two actual events or observations from your life) side by side, even though they might have been separated in actuality by months or years. That's fiction, too: the ordering of events.

So one can be honest without being truthful. One can be believable without being factual.

But remember what I said about believability. Maybe I'm just *saying* the above stories really happened so you'll believe me. Maybe Tony Turnbull is as much a fiction as Tony Trimball. Maybe I'm an incorrigible liar and need to seek therapy.

Maybe. I'm not telling.

I'm not trying to frustrate you or show you how clever I am. I'm just trying to make a point.

Gail Godwin, in her essay "Becoming a Writer," writes about some of the formative experiences of her life and how they shaped her as a fiction writer. Near the end of her essay, she writes:

> This account of my own unfolding as a writer has been the truth. But it is also full of lies, many of which I'm not

aware of. But in one sense, perhaps the most important, it is all true: it could have been written by nobody but me. What I have chosen to tell, how I have chosen to tell it, and what I have chosen not to tell, express me and the kind of writer I am.

If you want to write at all, whether from real life or not, you must be willing and able to use your imagination. That means you must be willing to take risks and sometimes look the fool. You must be willing to transform experience, not simply record it. If you were a good liar, daydreamer or troublemaker as a child, you'll probably make a good fiction writer. Daydreams, lies and trouble. That's the stuff of fiction.

CHAPTER ONE

Journals

To understand how to turn life into fiction, one must be observant. As a fiction writer, you try to convince the reader of the authenticity of the world you're creating, and that's why a journal comes in handy. Not every writer keeps a journal, and it's not necessary, but some writers find it invaluable. It's akin to an artist's sketchbook. It hones a writer's skills and makes him more observant. At parties, Victor Hugo used to stop conversations in midsentence, take a little notebook from his pocket and jot down what someone had said. A year later, the conversation would appear in his latest novel.

We're not talking about diaries here, though many writers have kept diaries. The diaries of Virginia Woolf and Anaïs Nin are widely considered works of art. There *is* some crossover between the subject matter of diaries and that of journals, but I see a diary as a day-to-day recording of existence, a reckoning of sorts, a justification of one's existence through a kind of chronicling that ends, ideally, at the end of one's life. Keeping a diary is certainly a creative act, but diaries are essentially private, although Thomas Mallon, in his book about people and their diaries, *A Book of One's Own* (Ticknor and Fields), convincingly argues that diaries do have an audience, whether one's future self, a friend or relative, or posterity.

Some people might find it crude to see one's experience as grist for the mill, and certainly if you go through life simply trying to figure out how to use every real-life experience in your fiction, then, emotionally and spiritually, you'll lead an impoverished existence. A certain amount of distance is necessary to write successfully about real life, and if you always maintain that distance, you're not really living your life to its fullest.

But nothing is wrong with jotting down a detail here and there, an overheard conversation, a memory that comes upon you, a dream. Some writers believe that if you can't remember something, it must not be important, so they see no use for a journal. Each to her own, but if I didn't have my journal with me the other day, I would have had nowhere to record the slogan I saw on a plumber's truck on the highway: "A good flush is better than a full house." Okay, it's corny, but I like a plumber with a sense of humor. Maybe I'll never use this slogan in a story. It doesn't matter. To me, there's something wonderful in simply recording this fragment of plumber wit.

Maybe someday I'll be writing a story with a plumber in it, and I'll think to myself, *What was that slogan I saw on the side of that plumber's truck that one time? Three of a kind are better than two pair? Nope, that wasn't it.* Luckily, I'll have my journal to flip through to refresh my memory. And in the process of flipping through my journals, I'll probably come across three or four other intriguing fragments or story ideas I've completely forgotten about.

WRITERS AND THEIR JOURNALS

I've kept a journal on a capricious basis since I was sixteen. For me, my journal is a supplement to my imagination. I recently heard of a novelist who cuts out magazine photos of people, pastes them on his study wall and uses them as the basis for his character descriptions. I completely approve. Writing is hard enough, and I welcome anything that helps me along. Besides, I can't help but filter what I see through my imagination, so even my most autobiographical fiction is, in a sense, wholly imagined.

As F. Scott Fitzgerald's career was waning, he not only recorded observations and ideas in his notebooks, he also purposefully set about "stripping" his unpublished short stories for phrases and descriptions he might later use in his novels. The entries were dutifully logged by his secretaries. This stripping down of stories for later use is by no means a terrible thing to do. Most writers cull phrases or paragraphs from failed stories for later use. It's just rare for a writer to be so deliberate about it.

The Austrian writer Peter Handke uses the journal form as an end in itself in his novel *The Weight of the World* (Farrar, Straus and Giroux). Critic June Schlueter writes of *The Weight of the World*:

> . . . Each entry stands as an independent fragment of experience. The seemingly random images, observations, memories, and thoughts of the journals . . . are held together only by the central consciousness of the author-narrator, who remembers and creates a melange of outer- and inner-world experiences, mingling present and past, real and surreal, convictions, speculations, impressions, and ideas.

I can't think of a more concise definition of a journal.

There's a certain random quality to a journal, or there should be. Absent from a journal is the deliberate, day-to-dayness of a diary. Part of the joy of keeping a journal lies in its randomness. It's your own personal *I Ching, or Book of Changes*. Instead of casting sticks to tell your future, you flip pages.

Here are a few randomly chosen excerpts from Peter Handke's *The Weight of the World*:

> Alone with the glugging of the dishwasher.

> "Are you disgusted with me?" "No, I knew what to expect."

> F. imitated my way of laughing: a malicious laugh which I hated in my father.

> Names are ridiculous. Why couldn't I have a number instead?

> The balloon vanishing over the treetops: so this is death, I thought for a moment.

Most of the book tends toward the morose and self-serious in this way. Nothing is wrong with that. With a title like *The Weight of the World*, you should have some idea of what you're wading into.

Allen Ginsberg's journals are a lot more whimsical, though still quite serious in their own way. In his journals of the early fifties and sixties, his musings often take on the tone of the satirist and gadfly:

Do big fat American people know their Seoul from a hole in the ground?

I can't even commit a crime with a Clean Conscience anymore.

"You're fighting problems that are outside your control — in this business (Dentistry) — you gotta outguess the factors that are involved." Meaning: my patients never brush their teeth properly.

"After I got thru living in Milwaukee . . . I developed a taste for Blatz."

Ginsberg even quotes from Kafka's diaries in his journals:

Feb. 25, 1912 — Hold fast to the diary from today on! Write regularly! Don't surrender! Even if no salvation should come, I want to be worthy of it every moment."

David Michael Kaplan, a short story writer and author of the novel *Skating in the Dark* (Pantheon), keeps a journal as a source for ideas for his fiction. Kaplan says, "My working method is to keep a journal, and I've been keeping a journal for God knows how many years, twenty years? I've got a whole shelf full. I couldn't work without them. Whenever there's something that grabs me, what I think of as the potential seed idea for a story, around which eventually other seed ideas will coalesce like a crystal, I copy it down in the journal. They can come from anywhere — a conversation I overhear, or something that I see in passing, or they can be something that I read in the newspaper, or an anecdote that somebody tells me, that might not be much in itself, but it has something there that interests me — or it can be something that directly happened to me. Anyway, all of these things are kind of in the air, they're floating around. They're there to be grabbed, and I find that if I don't grab them, if I don't write them down in this journal that goes everywhere with me, then they disappear. You don't remember. A lot of people might say the things that you don't remember aren't worth remembering anyway. The stuff that's important, that'll become a story eventually, you'll remember. But I don't think that's actually true. From my own experience it hasn't *been* true. Things that developed and became parts of stories of mine are things that I would not have remembered otherwise."

TRIGGERS

A journal is essentially the place we store triggers — things that have caught our attention and started our imaginations rolling. Anything can be a trigger for your imagination, from seeing a license plate (a story of David Michael Kaplan's, "Anne Rey," came from a chance spotting of a vanity license plate on an L.A. freeway) to an overheard snatch of dialogue. It's not important what the trigger is. What's important is that something gets your imagination going, allowing you to make that leap from fact to fiction — and also that you write it down.

The trigger for Sue Miller's wonderful story, "Inventing the Abbotts," which originally was titled "The Lover of Women," was a chance meeting with an old boyfriend. As she explains in the 1987 edition of *The Best American Short Stories*: "In July of 1983, while I was helping my father repair his house in the mountains, I ran into a man who'd been my first sweetheart in that summer place, when I was fourteen. We sat around together for a long, black-fly-ridden New Hampshire evening, talking about the various complications and joys and wrinkles of the intervening twenty-five years or so. In the course of the evening, he told me a story of dating all three sisters in a family we both knew, of running into the mother years later, of her saying curtly to him, 'Well, I've no more daughters for you.' That line seemed expressive of so much . . . that it stayed in my mind. . . .

"I had an office that year . . . with a large grassy yard behind it. Over the time I was working on 'The Lover of Women,' this yard was the site of several parties, and the band music floating across Brattle Street into my windows seemed part of what helped me write. . . .

"Even now [the story] seems a gift: the accident of meeting my old sweetheart, the wonderful line that triggered my imagination . . . the music that wound its way into it."

THE TRANSFORMATION PROCESS

It's not the material. It's how you write it. A friend once told me an anecdote that I wrote in my journal, not once but twice. I guess I forgot about the first entry.

> Scott told me of a couple of children, one white, one black, who were no more than five years old, and they were running around Boston Commons with a pizza box. They ran from one person to the next, saying, "You want a slice of pizza?" Then they opened the box. Inside, there was a squirrel that had been flattened by a car. They came up and did this to someone who was standing near Scott, and Scott yelled after them, "You kids should be ashamed of yourselves!"

I used this entry in a story, "Installations," about an unlikely affair between a conductor on the Chicago El and a fledgling performance artist named Ivy, who sees everything, all experience, as art. I have as much trouble with people like Ivy, who see everything as art, as I have with people who want "just the facts, ma'am," and feel that art is irrelevant.

I don't want to be self-aggrandizing here, but I want to show you how I transformed the passage. I used the basic idea of the squirrel in the pizza box, stretched it, dramatized it and altered it to fit the specifications of my story. In the following scene, my protagonist, the El conductor, has just been taken by Ivy to his first performance art exhibit, called an "installation," and he has no idea what to make of it. By the way, the description of the installation is a pretty accurate one of an actual installation I saw in Chicago while *I* was dating a fledgling performance artist, though her name wasn't Ivy and the similarities end there. I didn't, however, record the installation in my journal. It was so bizarre I knew I'd remember every detail for the rest of my life.

> We pass through a white curtain into this scene: a darkened room with a naked man and woman, thirtyish, lying like two sticks of old butter in the middle of the room. Either they're dead or mannequins. The music in the

room sounds like the part in *The Wizard of Oz* where Dorothy and her boyfriends are looking at the witch's castle, and the soldiers march around singing: "O-li-o-eyohhh-oh."

Ivy takes my hand and we approach the couple on the floor. A dozen other people saunter around as though nothing special's going on. We can't get any closer than five feet. The couple on the floor are surrounded by hundreds of apples in the shape of a cross. A ragged bat hangs above them, its ribbed wings stretching six feet. A sideways neon eight sways between the wings and glows pale blue.

This is what Ivy calls an installation. This is what I call a fun house.

Up close, I see their chests moving slightly, a small tremor from one of the woman's fingers touching the man's hand, a flickering eyelid. I study them and wonder if I've ever seen them on the El. I wonder if the woman's parents know this is what she does for a living.

Candles burn on their chests. Luckily the candles are in jars, or the wax would be excruciating. Still, the heat must get to them. Not that I can tell. They're not exactly your liveliest couple. I can imagine showing up at Angel's Shortstop, my neighborhood bar, with them stiff as corpses on the bar stools, the candles still stuck on their chests. Angel would serve them up a couple of Old Styles, and squint at me and say, "They friends of yours?"

Yeah, they're installations.

We take the El back to Belmont and walk over to Clark Street. Everything seems strange tonight: a man waiting in the window of a tattoo parlor, the moan coming out of a storefront church.

Ivy asks me what I think about the installations. I don't know. I haven't thought about it. What are you supposed to think about a naked man and woman with candles on their chests?

"Everything," she says. "Adam and Eve lying in suspended animation beneath death and infinity. Christ figures surrounded by the forbidden fruit."

Yeah, well, I guess.

We turn the corner of Clark and Belmont, and two kids, one black and one white, not more than nine years old, slam into us as they tear through the parking lot of Dunkin' Donuts.

"Hey, watch where you're going," I say, touching the white one lightly on the shoulder.

"You watch where you're going, you fag," the kid tells me.

The black kid has a pizza box in his hands. He smiles and says, "You want some pizza?"

"Yeah, you want some pizza?" says the white kid.

The black kid opens up the box. Inside is a squirrel, its head smashed, its legs stretched out, its belly split open. At least a hundred cars have run over it. As flat as a pizza. A circle of dried tomato paste surrounds the carcass.

Before I can react, the kids run off shouting and laughing. They block one pedestrian after another yelling, "Hey, you want some pizza? Free pizza."

Ivy picks up a soft drink cup from the sidewalk and throws it after them. The cup, plastic lid and straw still attached, falls to the ground three feet away.

"You brats," she screams. "Come back here."

Ivy takes off. The white kid trips. She chases the other one. I can't make out much through the distance and pedestrians. A few minutes later, she comes smiling back with the pizza box in her hands, the lid closed.

"What do you want *that* for?" I say.

"Stealing is the most sincere form of flattery," she says. "Picasso did it. Every great artist does it."

"Throw it away."

"Are you kidding?"

"Throw it away."

"Don't give me orders. I had to fight them for it."

I don't say a word. I'm tired of her. I was curious before, but now I'm just tired. I head for Angel's Short-stop and Ivy tags along. I figure it's Ivy's turn to feel out-of-place. Not many out-of-place people ever wander into Angel's. If they do, they wander back out again in a hurry. The crowd at Angel's is as tight as a VFW post.

Ignoring Ivy, I sit down on a stool at the bar. There isn't one for her, so she stands in between my stool and the next guy's, and places her pizza box on the counter. Angel gives her a look. Then she looks at me. I order a couple shots of Cuervo with Old Style chasers.

"I'll have to tap a new keg," says Angel. "How 'bout something else in the meantime?"

"How 'bout a mug of beefalo swill?" I say. "Come on, Angel. I'm talking brand loyalty."

"I'll go tap a new keg," she says. Angel is about sixty years old and has a white bubble hair-do. She comes to Chicago via the coal mines of Kentucky, and her husband's long-gone with black lung. Angel's jukebox has only the thickest country-and-western songs, with three exceptions: "A Cub Fan's Dying Prayer," Sinatra's version of "Chicago," and "Angel of the Morning." She's always pumping quarters painted with red fingernail polish into the jukebox and pushing those three tunes. I can't count the number of times I've come into The Shortstop and heard her belting, "Just call me angel of the morning, baby. Just one more kiss before you leave me, angel." She thinks of The Shortstop as a family establishment, even though I'd fall off my stool if I ever saw a family walk through the door. Maybe a family of cockroaches or sewer-bred alligators. Definitely not a family of mammals.

When Angel returns with the Old Styles, Ivy pushes hers away and says, "I don't drink alcohol."

"Angel, this is Ivy," I say. "She comes from Cody, Illinois, the beefalo capital of the Midwest. It's ten miles south of Beloit."

"Blech!" says Ivy.

"What?"

"Beloit. I grew up with the name. It sounds like a quarter being dropped in a toilet. Beloit . . . Besides, I live in Chicago now."

"Yeah, she's a performance artist," I tell Angel.

"Pleased to meet you," she says.

"You want some pizza?" Ivy says.

"No, she doesn't want any pizza," I say, and put my hand on the lid.

"Domino's?" Angel says.

"It's not pizza," I say. "It's a squirrel."

"A squirrel."

"Yeah, a dead one."

"Pepperoni," Ivy says. "You want to see it, Angel?"

"Sure, why not?"

"No, you don't want to see it," I say. My hand is still on the lid.

Ivy looks sideways at me and gives me a half-smile, a dare. Her look says "What's the big deal?" She's right. After all, Angel's not my mother.

With my job and all, I'm not easy to faze, but Ivy definitely fazes me. Not only her actions, but the way she dresses. An orange scarf as big as window drapes. Black fishnet stockings and metallic silver lipstick.

"You ever had squirrel?" says Angel. "Tastes just like chicken. Of course, there ain't as much meat on a squirrel."

"Do you always believe what you see, Angel?" Ivy says.

"Almost never," says Angel, leaning towards her, a look of concentration on her face. "A fella come in here the other day selling key chains. He had a metal man and a metal woman on the key chain, and when he wiggled a lever they started doing things. He said he had a whole trunkful in his car, and did I want to sell some on a card behind the counter? I said, 'Look around, this is a family place.' He said, 'You'd be surprised. People just love them. I've seen grandmas and young girls go crazy over them.' 'Yeah, well this is a gay bar, buddy,' I said. 'That's fine,' he said. 'I can take off the woman and put on another man. I already did that with one gay establishment. I'll put on dogs. I'll put on a man and a horse. Even two Japanese girls and a rhinoceros if that's what you want.

Whatever turns you on.' Some people just want to shock you. I could have called the cops, but I ignored him. Eventually, he just slithered back under his rock."

"You want some pizza?" Ivy says.

"Yeah, why not?" says Angel.

I take my hand off the lid and wait for Ivy to open up the box, but she doesn't move. What's she waiting for? I wonder if I'm going nuts. If Ivy's brainwashing me. I've known her two days, and suddenly I want to show Angel the dead squirrel in the pizza box.

"One object can have many functions," Ivy says. "Consider this pizza box. For you and me, it signifies food. For Rocky the squirrel, it's his final resting place. When you put the two together, it's repulsive. Why? Because food and death are opposites, right? No, not at all. Food and death go hand in hand, but our escapist society allows us to blithely ignore that fact. Hold the mayo, hold the lettuce, special orders don't upset us. Right, Angel? Next time you go to an open casket funeral, don't be surprised if you see a pizza with the works lying there."

I have a strange feeling in my mouth. My tongue seems to be getting bigger. I've gone through my whole life barely noticing my tongue, and now, all of a sudden, it seems humongous. I can't figure out where to place it. I try to settle it down by my cheek. I stick it between my teeth.

Angel tucks her chin into her neck.

My tongue has swollen to the size of a blimp.

Still, I manage to say to Angel, "Ya wa thom peetha?"

"Sure, why not?" she says.

I open up the box and Angel shrinks back.

She gives me a look and I can already tell that she's canceled me out as a regular. Now, I'm just another bar story: "You remember Rick? He came in here with a squirrel in a pizza box. Yeah, it was dead."

Now is that stealing? I don't think so. I took a bare-boned anecdote from my journal and stretched it. You, undoubtedly, would have taken the squirrel in the pizza box and done something completely different with the image. You might have focused on the two children or a character based on yourself in that situation.

The writer and teacher George Garrett did something similar with the image of a wedding cake in the middle of the road, an image that one of his students, Beverly Goodrum, came up with in a class. Based on Goodrum's story, he and radio commentator Susan Stamberg asked twenty-three writers, both well known and not (including Garrett and Goodrum), to each write a story based on this image. Of course, a central question in each story was, "What is a wedding cake doing in the middle of the road?" Their versions were broadcast on NPR and collected in an anthology titled — what else? — *The Wedding Cake in the Middle of the Road* (Norton).

It's not the material. It's what you do with it.

A lot of the craft of writing fiction is in one's ability to order the material at hand, whether autobiographical or not. The content of the story itself means nothing. The form you give it, the way you shape the material, is everything.

Still, it might be helpful to know what from the above passage really happened — where it came from. As I mentioned, the installation itself was something I actually saw, though in this case, I had no need of recording it in my journal. When I lived in Chicago, there was a neighborhood bar called Kaye's Dugout, and a woman like Angel tended bar there. I never knew much about Kaye (if that woman behind the bar was indeed Kaye), where she came from, or whether she'd ever been married. But it's true that a lot of ex-coal miners from Kentucky have, over the years, moved to Chicago, and that a number of them suffer from black lung. When I was writing about Angel, I remembered this and so this is the history I decided to give her.

It's also true that at the corner of Clark and Belmont, you can still find a Dunkin' Donuts. I believe the storefront church is still there on Belmont, but the last time I visited Chicago I noticed the tattoo parlor was gone. The neighborhood is gentrifying.

Another real-life episode was the encounter with the man selling the funny key chains. That, too, happened, though not at Kaye's Dugout. It was at a more upscale fern bar in the area. This was something I recorded in my journal. It happened in midafternoon on a hot summer day in Chicago. I'd stopped in for a beer and was sitting at the bar when I overheard the man with the key chains trying to convince the bartender to sell some of them behind the bar.

I didn't record the conversation as it happened, but I wrote it down a short while later at my apartment. Almost everything Angel said in my story is verbatim what I overheard the man tell the bartender at the fern bar. However, there was more to that scene than what I chose to include in my story. Only the key chain episode fit in. Here's how the journal entry reads in its entirety.

6/10/86

Today, the humidity was about 70 percent. I walked all over town, and by the time I got off the Southport El I was drenched, so I stopped off for a beer at Justin's, a polished wood/ceiling fan kind of bar across from the station. An acquaintance, a guy named Carl, was tending bar, so I sat up at the counter, ordered an Augsburger. Carl started chatting with me, but as he was opening the bottle, it slipped out of his hands and he dropped it on the floor, beer splattering the front of his shirt. He said, "This hasn't been my day at all, man," and went to the rest room to wash the beer off. After he returned, neither of us had much to say to each other. Instead, he started flipping channels with the remote control for the two bar TVs, one at either end.

"Donahue," he said to me.

He kept the sound off one of the TVs, and that was the one I watched. I tried imagining the sound from the Donahue program to the other TV. The guests on Donahue were an unwed couple whose baby needed a heart transplant. The other TV had a burger commercial with talking burger cartons. Or, at least I assumed they were talking, since the burger boxes were flipping up and down in imitation of conversation. I listened to Donahue for a minute, placing the voices of the couple in the burger boxes. (Maybe I was suffering from heat stroke. I can't help editorializing there. Such a weird thing to do).

After the commercial was over, I turned back to Carl, who wasn't looking at Donahue, but talking to three guys at the bar. The one closest to me had a long, stubbly face. The man in the middle was dark-skinned, Hispanic, and the guy at the end wore a green Justin's T-shirt with a dog mascot on front. This man looked large and boyish.

"So I guess I'm moving to North Carolina," I told Carl, loud enough for everyone to hear.

Carl turned toward me and said, "No kidding." He looked surprised.

For some reason, I thought I had mentioned it to him before.

"Yeah, I got a job there."

"You ever been to North Carolina?" the man with the stubble asked me. He had a hard tone in his voice, as though he was talking about prison.

"Yeah," I said.

"Oh," he said. He took a sip of his beer and said, "I've been there."

The phone rang and the man with the stubble said, "I bet that's Justin."

"Justin hates me," said the Hispanic man.

Carl looked over at the man with the stubble, who said, "He's a real obnoxious son of a bitch, but he mellows out once you get to know him," and he pointed at the Hispanic guy.

Carl went to the phone and the Hispanic man laughed and yelled after him, "Tell Justin that Mexican son of a bitch is here. Yeah, he *hates* me."

Carl picked up the phone and took it around the corner, speaking softly.

The three men at the counter looked at each other and broke out laughing.

"It *is* him," said the Hispanic man.

"Don't worry," said the guy with the stubble. "Carl can handle it. He's a good guy."

Carl hung up and started talking to the three guys again.

"Do you like working here?" I asked Carl.

"Yeah, I love it," he said. "But the hours are catching

up with me. I opened this morning and closed last night."

Carl looked past me toward the door. A man in his fifties walked in wearing oily brown polyester pants.

Carl went to the middle of the bar and leaned forward.

"Can I help you?"

"Yeah, is Justin here?"

"No, he won't be in till six. Can I help you?"

Well, I wanted to see if he'd be interested in buying some of these," and he took out a key chain from his pocket. The key chain had two metal figures attached to it, a man and a woman. The guy in the brown pants wiggled a little lever.

Carl took it from the man and wiggled the lever himself. Then he brought it to the end of the bar and showed it to the three guys there.

"Justin will love this," said the man with the stubble.

"How much you want for this?" asked the Hispanic man.

"Well, I'm asking three," said the man, who had now positioned himself between me and the other three men. "But I'll take two."

The Hispanic man who was holding the key chain laughed. The guy with the stubble whipped out his wallet and threw two dollars at the man.

"Justin'll love this," he said. "It's the perfect present for him."

"I got more in my car," said the man. "Who else wants one?"

"No, that's all," said the man with the stubble.

Then he took out another dollar bill and threw it at the man. "Here, it's worth three," he said.

"I got a whole load of them in my trunk," said the man. "It's right around the corner. I've got thousands."

"One's plenty," said the man with the stubble.

"But I was thinking of giving you a bunch to sell on a card behind the bar."

The four other guys laughed and the man with the stubble said, "Not here. That wouldn't go here."

"You'd be surprised," said the man. "People just love

them. I've seen women and young girls go crazy over them."

"Yeah, well this is a gay bar," said the guy with the stubble, and the other guys laughed.

"That's fine," said the man. "I can take off the woman and put on another man. I already did that for one gay bar."

"What about dogs?" said the Hispanic man. "I want one with a man and a dog."

"Fine. I can put on anything."

"Well, I want two Japanese girls and a rhinoceros," said the Hispanic man.

"I want a man and a horse," said the guy with the stubble.

"Sure, whatever you want," said the man.

"This is all we want," said the man with the stubble. "You'll have to go somewhere else."

The man laughed and started walking out. "Anything you want," he said. "Well, I'll be back tonight to see Justin."

"No, don't come back," said the man with the stubble.

"Yeah, come back," said the Hispanic man. "Justin likes your element."

After the man was gone, the guy with the stubble said, "Did you see that guy's pants? I would have given him three dollars for those pants."

I love those characters, and I love some of their lines. I like the whole scene, in fact. The personalities seem pretty distinct to me. I love that line, "Justin likes your element." Too bad I couldn't use more of the scene in my story. Note, I referred to these guys as characters, not people. They *are* people. But the journal entry isn't flesh and blood. I couldn't reproduce real people in flesh and blood, in all their complexity, even if I wanted to. With the exception of Carl, I met them once and wouldn't know them again if I saw them. I can only imagine. That, again, is the key word. Imagine. Once you set pen to paper, even in your journal, your imagination plays an important role. There's no such thing as objectivity, as any basic philosophy course will tell you. Everything is a matter of perceptions. You'd write down the above incident in a different way from the way I wrote it. The words you'd choose would be different. What you thought was important would be different. You might not even see the scene as important at all. You might forget it entirely. But as soon as you started recording it, you'd be using your imagination.

That might sound like a great rationalization. Obviously, you can't go around thinking of everyone as a character. There are limits. All I'm saying is that your journal is your sketchbook. Don't think of it as a diary. As I mentioned, I wrote all of this down after I returned home. I have a good memory, but I can't swear that every word I recorded in my journal was exactly the way it was uttered. Does it matter? I don't think so. It's your journal. You're a fiction writer, not a reporter. Nineteenth-century English poet and critic Matthew Arnold said, "Journalism is literature in a hurry." Don't be in a hurry. Play around with it. You don't have to try to be faithful to reality in your journal. You couldn't be, even if you tried.

In any case, what I used from that journal entry was only a smidgen of the scene. Notice that in my journal entry I hardly paid any attention to the third guy, the one with the Justin's T-shirt. In a story, I'd probably cut him out or give him a larger role. Everything in fiction counts, and that's not always the case in real life. In real life, there are people who sit at the end of the bar without a role to play. In fiction, a character is either necessary to the story or extraneous.

In "Installations," none of those guys was necessary. I used the key chain incident itself and I condensed what the men at the bar said and attributed their whimsical requests to the key chain man. Then I further removed the scene from real life by filtering the dialogue through Angel's perceptions. As much as I liked some of those other passages in the journal, I had to be careful to use only what fit into my story, no more, no less.

What would have happened to the story if I'd simply lifted the entire journal entry into my story without transforming it? What would have happened if I'd included Carl, the Hispanic man, the guy with the stubble, the guy with the Justin's T-shirt *and* the key chain? Obviously, the story would have become unfocused. We'd forget about Ivy and Rick, not to mention Angel. In a later chapter we'll discuss strategies for focusing stories like this that are based in real life.

One thing you must understand as a fiction writer: Real life matters only as a conduit for your imagination. As a fiction writer, your imagination takes precedence. As a human being, life takes precedence over your imagination, and it's best not to confuse the two.

One other journal entry found its way into the squirrel in the pizza box scene, and that was the mention of Rick's tongue suddenly seeming large. A friend once told me that an acquaintance of his had one day stopped midsentence and said, "You know, all of a sudden I'm noticing my tongue. I've gone through my whole life without noticing it, but now I can't figure out where to place it in my mouth. It keeps getting in the way." My friend laughed and said, "Maybe you should seek therapy."

When I came to the climax of the scene, when Rick finally decided to show Angel the squirrel in the pizza box, I wanted to show a change in him, a change in his perceptions, a hint that he was going through almost physical changes because of his association with Ivy. That's when I remembered the man who didn't know where to put his tongue.

Many passages in my journal are irrelevant and will never find their ways into stories. I don't even know what some of the passages mean.

At the end of the Justin's entry, there are three lines that make little sense to me:

> Maybe follows him out to car?
> Something about his move, his girlfriend.
> "Why are you trying to alienate me?" Mother asks.

I may have been thinking of a story. Judging from the strength of those lines, I wisely abandoned the idea.

Some of my journals contain these kinds of lines, indecipherable and abandoned ideas and passages. I also have grocery lists, quotes from other writers and artists, phone numbers, addresses. And, of course, I've included notes to myself on where to proceed in my novel or short stories, such as:

Henry feels threatened by Gail, but he can't leave. He feels at home here. It *is* his home. Still, he feels compelled to redeem himself, to prove himself. Gail thinks Henry's clumsy, wimpish, impotent, unmasculine. He decides to take action. He needs to show Gail she's wrong.

There used to be an element of the macho in Henry.

Henry needs to be less passive.

Bring back Sid.

Henry and Willy have bidding war at auction. Henry suddenly gets aggressive, but the fact that he gets car might redeem himself in Gail's eyes.

Basically, stage directions. Then there are the story ideas:

About Al at Our Place. How I thought he was brilliant and wanted to be just like him, but then we, the regulars of Our Place, decided he was really mad, and this diminished him as a human being.

This is more or less indecipherable to you and probably doesn't seem like much of an idea at all. But *I* know what I'm referring to, and in a journal that's all that counts.

I don't include anecdotes in my journals with the intention of putting them in future stories. It's not that calculated. I write something down because it grabs my attention, because I'd hate for it to be lost. For instance, there was the time a local theater critic came to one of my classes and told us about an amateur production of *Amadeus* in which everything went wrong:

Perry Tannenbaum came to my Review Writing class today and he told us a story about reviewing a local production of *Amadeus*. Apparently, they got everything wrong. First of all, the guy playing Salieri had never acted before. Halfway through the play, he forgot his lines and ran offstage. Then, during the scene in which *The Magic Flute* premieres, something went wrong with the sound and there was just silence as the courtiers applauded. Then, at the end of the play, as Mozart lay dying, he was supposed to have a vision of his father appearing in the door wearing his three-cornered hat while portentous music played. Instead, when they cued the sound, the light, airy music of *The Magic Flute* started playing when his father, dressed in black, appeared in the doorway and glowered.

I doubt this entry will ever find its way into a story of mine, but who knows? I wrote it down simply because it was funny. But now that I think about it, I can see it working into a story in a couple of ways. The way in which I'd incorporate the anecdote would depend entirely on whose point of view the story is told from. The haughty critic would view the episode differently from the unfortunate amateur thespian who played Salieri.

I keep a journal for a variety of reasons. Sometimes I want to chronicle, as in a diary. Sometimes I want to record a detail that otherwise would be lost forever. Like David Michael Kaplan, sometimes I record a dream, and a couple of these dreams have actually been the kernels for some short stories I've written.

Whatever the case, it's important to write in your journal before the event or image becomes stale. We've all had dreams that have awakened us in the middle of the night, that seem so striking we want to record them. But we're tired and want to go back to sleep. We say, "Oh, I'll write it down in the morning when I wake up." Almost invariably, when we awake in the morning, the dream has disappeared. So we rationalize further. "Oh, it probably wasn't that interesting anyway." But what if it was?

Of course, what's worth noting in your journal is up to you. But I'd suggest carrying a small notebook with you at all times, one that can fit in your pocket or purse. Don't go anywhere without it, and take along a pen that works. As Thoreau wrote, "The writer who postpones the recording of his thoughts uses an iron which has cooled to burn a hole with." That's a quote I wrote down in one of my journals.

Writers are spies, liars and thieves. Some, like Jean Genet, have been real criminals; some, like Graham Greene, have actually been spies. But most are spies and thieves in a more general sense. Your journal is basically your spy notebook. Don't let it fall into enemy hands. Greene used his journals extensively to write *The Heart of the Matter* (Viking Penguin) and *A Burnt-Out Case* (Viking Penguin).

Later, we'll discuss ethics, but remember, you're writing fiction. There's nothing wrong with borrowing from real life. It's neither crass nor unimaginative unless one goes about it in a crass or unimaginative way. *Imagination comes in the ordering of events, not in their source.*

WEAVING JOURNAL ENTRIES INTO FICTION

Writing is an associative process. And fiction writing is a kind of mosaic, a piecing together of memory and imagination. One's journal can come in handy in this way, but I don't want to give you the impression that I simply flip through my journal, filling in the blanks with fun-filled episodes from real life until I have enough pages to call it a story. It's not a matter of simply dropping overheard bits of conversation into a story. I wish it was that easy. One must attempt to weave in what one uses.

For instance, here's a bit of overheard dialogue from Fitzgerald's notebook: "He wants to make a goddess out of me and I want to be Mickey Mouse."

In the completed story, "On Your Own," which was published posthumously, the Mickey Mouse quote isn't dropped in casually. On the contrary, it's woven seamlessly into the story, which concerns a young actress named Evelyn who's returning by boat to America after a five-year absence and some success on the British stage. On the voyage, she becomes entangled with a rich young lawyer named George Ives. The story was rejected seven times by various magazines, something Fitzgerald wasn't used to. Fitzgerald thought it was his one unpublished story with that "one little drop of something . . . the extra I had."

Early in the story, after the young couple meet, they walk the deck together:

> "You were a treat," he said. "You're like Mickey Mouse."
>
> She took his arm and bent double over it with laughter.
>
> "I like being Mickey Mouse . . ."

Later, after an on-again, off-again romance (and after Evelyn discovers George is rich), they have the following exchange:

"Would you consider marrying me?"
"Yes, I'd consider marrying you."
"Of course if you married me we'd live in New York."
"Call me Mickey Mouse," she said suddenly.
"Why?"
"I don't know—it was fun when you called me Mickey Mouse."

A little silly, but then, Evelyn is a little silly. That night, she wonders what she's gotten herself into:

"He wants to make a goddess out of me and I want to be Mickey Mouse."

Finally, George's mother, a wealthy society matron, invites Evelyn to dinner. At the dinner party is a certain Colonel Cary, who Evelyn has met before—under slightly darker circumstances. It turns out that when she was a starving young actress on Broadway and had to go for days without eating, she survived by being a "party girl." Intimidated by Colonel Cary's presence, Evelyn gets drunk on champagne, blabs everything and lashes out at George's mother, who's properly horrified but tries to put a good face on things. Of course, George, under his mother's wing all along, tries to dump Evelyn, who, in her world-weary fashion, takes it all with philosophical aplomb.

Ah, well, maybe she'd better go back to England—and be Mickey Mouse. He didn't know anything about women, anything about love, and to her that was the unforgivable sin.

Fiction, unlike real life, demands a kind of *symmetry*, or balance. No phrase or image or overheard bit of dialogue should be wasted or thrown carelessly into a story or novel. There's an old dramatic trick here that Fitzgerald has employed: If you want a reader to pay special attention to an image, put it in not once or twice, but three times. The first time you make a reference to Mickey Mouse, the reader will hardly notice. The second time, the reader's subconscious takes note, but it barely registers on the reader's conscious mind. The third time is the charm. In this case, Mickey Mouse becomes an organic symbol of Evelyn's frivolity, as well as her vacuousness. Fitzgerald has taken this overheard dialogue and fashioned it to suit his characters and their situation.

Fitzgerald also wrote ideas for short stories in his notebooks, including the following one, based on a true story:

> There once was a moving picture magnate who was shipwrecked on a desert island with nothing but two dozen cans of film (Herbert Howe).

As far as I know, Fitzgerald never did anything with the idea. I've thought about it myself. It's intriguing, but it's sort of a one-joke story, the idea of the creator stranded with nothing but potential, and without the means to do anything about it. The fact that Fitzgerald never did anything with the idea is all the more fitting. We all have canisters of film that we'll never develop.

The point is that a journal entry is little but a raw piece of information. What you do with it later is the tricky part. For the time being, enjoy yourself. Whoop it up. Have a party in your journal. Your journal entries can be more or less formless. They can be ungrammatical. You may misspell all the words you like. They can make no sense at all. There'll be enough time later for biting your fingernails to the quick, gnashing your teeth and beating your breast in frustration — once you decide to develop your ideas into a story or a novel.

Exercises

Journals aren't only repositories for overheard conversations, but places to experiment, to recall a scene from your childhood, to try out first lines. A fiction writer, or any artist, attempts to see the world in a new light, in a way that makes the ordinary seem extraordinary (or the extraordinary seem ordinary). Simply paying attention to the everyday world around you will soon yield extraordinary results.

1. Go to a park or a shopping mall or somewhere else where people congregate in large numbers. Sit on a bench with your journal and sketch the people walking by — not with pictures but words. Describe at least three people in as much detail as possible: their gestures, what they're wearing, what they're saying. Try not to pass judgment on the people you're observing. Let the descriptions do all the talking.

2. Close your eyes. Remember a scene from your childhood. It doesn't have to be a traumatic event or something inherently dramatic. In fact, it's best to simply go with the first memory that surfaces. Remember all its details. Use the senses. If you remember making orange peel candy with your grandmother, imagine the smells of the orange rinds, the sight of the curled crisp rinds, smothered in sugar, and baking. The ones that invariably burned, but your grandmother liked those, right? Or maybe she just said she liked them so you could have the ones that came out perfect. What did they taste like? What did you and your grandmother talk about? Try to evoke the memory with as much clarity as possible. Now write it down in your journal. It doesn't have to fit into a story. It's just practice. But if it *does* fit into a story, that's fine, too. I once had a teacher who said he didn't understand when people said they had nothing to write about. All they have to do is keep their eyes open and/or remember.

3. Eavesdrop on a couple of strangers. (Don't be obvious. I don't want you to end up in jail.) Again, this is just practice, so don't worry about it. Write down what they say as close to verbatim as possible. Do you notice any difference between the conversation you've recorded and the dialogue of short stories and novels? Generally, fiction writers try to make their dialogue seem as realistic as possible. The key word is "seem." Dialogue also has to flow smoothly. In real life, people stutter, say "ah" and "um," change subjects midsentence, ramble, pay no attention at all to what the other person is saying, trail off, talk at the same time. To a certain degree, this can be imitated in one's fictional dialogue, and it can even heighten humor or tension. Film director Robert Altman has been playing with the way people really speak for a quarter of a century. Look at *M*A*S*H* or *Nashville* and notice how often characters speak at the same time. It's intriguing. It's funny. And it's often darned annoying. If you try to be too true (recording dialect *exactly*, printing every "um,") you risk losing your readers, making them stumble over awkward phrases and misspellings—in short, making them conscious that they are reading a story. That's the last thing you want to do. You don't want to call attention to the fact that what you've written isn't real. You want to seduce readers into believing they have entered a world as real as the one they inhabit every day. Paradoxically, that often means not being absolutely realistic with one's dialogue. A good rule of thumb: If it's going to jar readers and make them stumble, cut it out.

4. Here are a few of Fitzgerald's ideas from his notebooks. See where you can go with them. Remember, it's just practice, and it's not how he would have written them anyway. Identify which ideas have the best story potential, and which seem like they won't lead anywhere. Which ones seem too limited? Too open-ended?

> Story about a man trying to live down his crazy past and encountering it everywhere.

> Play about a whole lot of old people—terrible things happen to them and they don't really care.

> The Dancer Who Found She Could Fly

A young woman bill collector undertakes to collect a ruined man's debts. They prove to be moral as well as financial.

Flower shop, Bishop, Malmaison, Constantine, clinics, black men, nurses.

Words.

5. Think back within the last year or so and remember dealing with a service person — a plumber, an air duct specialist, a mechanic. Remember the details. Write them down in your journal. What was he wearing? Was he wearing a toupee? A high school ring? Did he tell you about his love of tying lures and fishing off of Cape Hatteras? Or volunteering to catch and tag sharks for scientists? Was he a she? Life is in the details, and so is good fiction. Often when one imagines something whole cloth (that is, *without* incorporating bits of one's own observations and experience), one comes up with a stereotype or cliché. If you want to write a story about a plumber, the first images that spring to mind are sometimes the most hackneyed. Rely less on your preconceptions and more on your own experience with plumbers or service people of *any* kind.

CHAPTER TWO

Finding Your Form

Perhaps everyone has a story to tell, but many never get around to telling them, and many others tell them poorly. Many people have led fascinating lives but falter when they attempt to tell their stories. Often, this is because they focus on content rather than form. There's a difference between a memoir and a novel. A memoir is supposed to be true. A novel isn't. The difference between fact and fiction. As flip as that might sound, it's a complex distinction, and some writers blur the distinction to good effect. Others, claiming they want to write fiction, really want to write memoirs. If you base a story on an actual event but refuse to alter it because "that's the way it really happened," you probably want to write a memoir instead of a story. I'm going to assume that you're here to write fiction transformed from fact rather than unadulterated fact. Still, I think it would be worthwhile to discuss some of the various forms and distinctions between them before moving on.

I don't want to be unfair to memoir writers, since such writing is much more involved than simply setting down an event as it happened. Who knows how it happened? Can you trust your eyes, your memory? Does your father remember it differently from you? Had you been drinking that night? Where do you begin to relate the event? The night before, when Joey called you and invited you out skinny-dipping, and you had to think of an excuse to tell your dad? Maybe you want to start in the tepid waters of the lake instead. Or maybe you want to begin that chapter of your memoir in a more reflective way. "Some people would undoubtedly say that I was a brat when I was a young 'un. . . ." And what about word choice and diction? You really want to use the words "young 'un" and "undoubtedly" in the same sentence? And who really cares about your skinny-dipping episode in 1966? Was it so amazing that it's going to work as the centerpiece of your memoir, *Treading Water in the Sixties*?

"Okay," you say, slightly insulted. "If not a memoir, I'll make it a novel."

Not so fast.

Writing a novel is no easier than writing a memoir. Fiction writers must be flexible with their lives, write about "what if" rather than "what is." Writers need distance from events to write about them as fiction, to accept that these real events might not work in the story. And it's more important for the story to work than for it to be true (in the narrow sense of that word).

MEMOIRS, NOVELS AND ROMANS À CLEF

A memoir, as I said, is not simply a recording of events. That kind of recording, in its simplest form, is a diary (and that point is probably debatable, too). All types of writing have accepted forms and conventions. Letters, for instance, begin with "Dear" and end with "Love," "Best Wishes," "Truly" or some other appropriate word. Newspaper stories often use the inverted pyramid form. Short stories generally involve some kind of conflict, crisis and resolution.

A memoir takes a certain amount of arrogance to write (not that I'm suggesting this is one of its conventions). One must think one's life important or interesting enough to palm off on an unsuspecting public. At least fiction writers have the pretense that their work has more to do with their characters than with themselves. Still, I doubt you'd find much of a difference between a memoir writer and a fiction writer in the humility department.

Or maybe memoir writers tend more toward exhibitionism, are more willing — eager, in fact — to slap their cards on the table and squawk, "Read 'em and weep." The fiction writer, cagier, plays his hand close to his vest, pretends he knows how to bluff.

If you slosh your life down on the page, beginning with "I was born in . . ." and ending with, "As I pen these immortal words, I gasp my last breaths," what you've probably got is a self-indulgent autobiography, not a memoir. A memoir usually deals with a portion of one's life — say, childhood — not the life in its entirety. Like a novel, the art is in the ordering of events, not the events themselves. Sometimes what's called a memoir and what's labeled a novel seems due more to the whims of a publisher's marketing department than to any true distinction. In such cases, perhaps the best solution is the one Frederick Exley came up with in his book, *Fan's Notes* (Random House), which he subtitled *A Fictional Memoir*.

One distinction we can make is between simple memoirs and sophisticated ones. Celebrity tell-all books will continue to be printed by the hundreds of thousands as long as there remain virgin forests worth pulping for that glorious purpose.

One of the best memoirs to come along in recent years is Tobias Wolff's *This Boy's Life* (Atlantic Monthly Press). The book recalls Wolff's childhood, growing up in the Pacific Northwest in the fifties with his divorced mother, who marries a tyrannical and oafish man named Dwight. Wolff's brother, Geoffrey, has also written an excellent memoir, *The Duke of Deception* (Random House), about growing up on the opposite coast with the boys' con artist of a father.

This Boy's Life seems as much an autobiographical novel as a memoir. In fact, Wolff originally envisioned the book as a novel, but then decided against a fictional approach. I have a good memory and can recall dreams I had when I was three years old, but Wolff reaches back nearly forty years and fishes out whole conversations time and again. The fact is that all writing—whether a letter, a memoir or a novel—requires some artifice. And the act of writing down memories changes them. They become more real. The line blurs between actual memory and reconstructed written memory so that the writer is less and less able to know for certain what *really* happened. Perhaps Wolff has a photographic memory, or whatever the audio version of that would be, but I doubt it. Most likely, events and conversations much like the ones Wolff reproduces took place. Or perhaps several remarks were said at different times and Wolff patched them together to keep the story cohesive. Or maybe the conversations, some of them at least, never took place at all. So does that make Wolff a liar, or worse yet, a fiction writer? Well, he is a fiction writer of some note, and such impulses die hard.

Michael Caton-Jones, the director of the film version of *This Boy's Life*, says that during filming (in the town of Concrete, Washington, where Wolff grew up), people kept approaching him to give their own versions of events. But he fended all of them off. "Everybody's memory plays tricks, to be honest," he says. "I never let the truth get in the way of a good story, if I can help it." A man after my own heart.

The only character in the book that Caton-Jones found a little shadowy and wanted a better handle on, according to a *New York Times* article, was Wolff's mother, whom Wolff handled "with kid gloves." So naturally, he went to *The Duke of Deception*, where he found what he considered a more realistic portrait of her.

Here's a scene between Dwight and young Toby (or Jack, as he preferred to be called). In it, Dwight has just run over a beaver on the road on purpose and now stops to pick it up so he can sell the pelt. Notice how detailed the description is. Does it sound like a memory from forty years back? Are your memories this detailed?

> "Pick it up," Dwight told me. He opened the trunk of the car and said, "Pick it up. We'll skin the sucker out when we get home."
>
> I wanted to do what Dwight expected me to do, but I couldn't. I stood where I was and stared at the beaver.
>
> Dwight came up beside me. "That pelt's worth fifty dollars, bare minimum." He added, "Don't tell me you're afraid of the damned thing."
>
> "No sir."
>
> "Then pick it up." He watched me. "It's dead, for Christ's sake. It's just meat. Are you afraid of hamburger? Look." He bent down and gripped the tail in one hand and lifted the beaver off the ground. He tried to make this appear effortless but I could see he was surprised and strained by the beaver's weight. A stream of blood ran out of its nose, then stopped. A few drops fell on Dwight's shoes before he jerked the body away. Holding the beaver in front of him with both hands, Dwight carried it to the open trunk and let go. It landed hard. "There," he said, and wiped his hands on his pants leg.

Of course, that's an event one might remember verbatim, but this memoir is full of such events, all finely detailed. I'm not in any way trying to pull the curtain on the Wizard of Oz here. *This Boy's*

Life is a remarkable book, and perhaps Wolff does remember every detail from his childhood with clarity. But as far as I'm concerned, the point is not whether every detail is completely accurate or each word recorded on Memorex. The point is, is it a good story? Does it say something true about human relationships, about our tentative place in the world? Does it evoke a time and place outside of our own? If the answer to these questions is yes, I don't care whether it's called a memoir or a novel.

Making Distinctions

So what's the distinction between novels and memoirs? One good one is that not all novels deal with real life, while all memoirs ostensibly do. Plenty of science fiction and fantasy novels are out there, but no science fiction memoirs as far as I know, unless you count the works of Carlos Castaneda, published in the seventies, which recount his professedly true adventures with a mystical Indian named Don Juan. They're not exactly science fiction, but they're pretty wild.

Many people in the past have written thinly veiled tell-all books disguised as fiction. They're called romans à clef. In the late seventies, Truman Capote was working on one about Hollywood, called *Answered Prayers* (Random House), and an excerpt was published in *Esquire*. Half of his friends disowned him because he'd told a lot of secrets about their lives. He uncovered a lot of dirt. His defense was pretty valid: His former friends told him these stories freely at parties, in the presence of others, knowing all along that he was a writer. "What did they think I was?" he asked with a mixture of hurt and acidity, "the court jester?"

Making the commitment to write a novel can be intimidating. When I was in graduate school at the Iowa Writers' Workshop, many students were afraid to say they were working on a novel. Instead, they'd say, "I'm working on something longer." And that's pretty much how I feel.

The late author Norma Klein once said that to begin her first novel, she didn't think of it as a novel. She told herself she would write ten pages a day about a certain group of people over a certain amount of time, and after three hundred pages, she would see what she had written. She also didn't allow herself to go back and correct more than five pages from the previous day's work.

As far as I'm concerned, Klein's model is a good one. After you've written two hundred or so pages, it's a novel. It might not be a good one. It might not be published. It's longer than a story or a novella, so what else can it be? A memoir?

Still, I know I'm begging the question. According to writer David Shields, novels in general tend to be more concerned with story, while memoirs tend to focus more on an exploration of identity. That's not to say that novels are *always* more concerned with story, while memoirs are *always* more concerned with an exploration of identity, just that those are the tendencies.

In Shields' case, he's noticed his work steadily creeping away from fiction into the realm of nonfiction. His first novel, *Heroes* (Viking), about a midwestern basketball player and the reporter obsessed with him, is, more or less, a story he imagined whole cloth. His next novel, *Dead Languages* (Knopf), a widely praised novel about a boy who stutters, contains many elements of autobiography. As a child, Shields had a serious stuttering problem, but the story is almost entirely fiction. *A Handbook for Drowning* (Knopf), a story collection, is a step closer to autobiography—a few of the pieces feel, to Shields, almost like essays even if most of the details are imagined. His latest work, *Remote* (Knopf), is a series of fifty-two interconnected prose meditations. It is unquestionably a work of nonfiction. To Shields, the prose pieces coalesce into a kind of oblique autobiography. In this book, the author "reads his own life as though it were an allegory, an allegory about remoteness." Despite the autobiographical nature of the book, Shields still thinks the persona that emerges on the page is essentially a fictional character. "The identity I've evoked," he explains, "the voice I've used, the tone I've maintained, the details I've chosen, are highly selective, and in many instances, frankly fictionalized. To me, these definitions get pretty murky. Memory is a dream machine. The moment you put words on paper, the fiction-making begins."

But the question remains, *How do you decide on a novel or a memoir?* To a large degree, that's an individual decision, based on who you are and what your material is. Shields tells his students to ask themselves, "What is it you're trying to get to? Are you essentially trying to tell a story, and if so, are you interested in setting that story in some kind of place? Then you are probably working on a novel. But if the real impulse is a kind of excavation of a self, a kind of meditation on the self, are you really working on a memoir or autobiography of some kind?" When Shields began working on *Remote*, he thought it was going to be a novel. "After a while, though, I realized I wasn't interested in character conflict per se. And I wasn't interested in a physical place, though I made gestures in those directions. What I was interested in was more autobiographical: the revelation of a psyche's theme via a sequence of tightly interlocking prose riffs, which became the book."

Story or plot as defined by character conflict seems to be the main distinction we can make here. Story involves a cause/effect relationship—that is, the character and her motivations are generally what fuels the story and its attendant conflict. A memoir proceeds perhaps more as memory does, in brief, episodic flashes illuminated by an overall picture of a central consciousness. Of course, memoir and fiction often bleed into each other, as we've already discussed, so these are not firm distinctions. Memoirs often contain conflict, as in Tobias Wolff's conflict with his stepfather, and fiction will often be concerned with an uncovering of the self in the context of world surrounding the self—as in much of the work of Milan Kundera.

Let's take the discussion down a few notches and ask ourselves some questions that are perhaps more pedestrian, but no less important.

Ask yourself how wedded you are to the facts of the story. Must you stay true to the core of the initial experience? Must you convey the whole of that experience? If you can't bear changing even the name of your grade school teacher, you might want to write a memoir, and you should find a book on memoir writing.

Why do you want to write this memoir in the first place? To get something off your chest? That might be good for you on a personal level, but that's not a good reason for anyone else reading your book.

The nature of the material itself rarely provides much help in deciding between a memoir and a novel. The most unusual story might make a terrible novel or memoir. The most ordinary story (growing up in Concrete, Washington) can be turned into a moving and artful memoir. The secret is in the ability and concerns of the writer, not in the material. Fiction writers sometimes pretend that their imagined writing is actually nonfiction or that their nonfiction is actually imagined, but these are simply tricks and subterfuges. Calling a story true if the writing isn't believable might fool most of the people most of the time, but not all of the people all of the time. Likewise, couching a nonfiction story in fictional terms won't necessarily stop you from being sued—but more on that in a later chapter.

Here's a note for beginning writers. If you haven't written much before your attempt to write your memoirs or your autobiographical novel, it would be a good idea to get some training. That you know how to write doesn't automatically mean you can write well yet. Think how absurd it would be for a cello student, after learning how to hold the bow and play the scales, to immediately audition for first cello in the New York Philharmonic. Like any craft, writing fiction or nonfiction well often takes a long apprenticeship. The first thing you should do is read as many memoirs or novels as you can, and at the same time, enroll in a local creative writing class at a university or community college. Don't tell your teacher that the only reason you're in the class is so you can write your memoirs or the great American novel. Put it aside for the time being. Write a lot. Listen to the comments of your classmates and your teacher. Take the same class again or move to the next level. I bet your conception of the book will change entirely.

ANECDOTES AND SHORT STORIES

I heard an anecdote once that a woman I know swore was true. It concerned a woman in a small town in Scotland who was a social climber. She decided to have a party and invite the elite of her town so she could rub elbows with them: the doctors, the lawyers, the editor of the newspaper. One of the dishes she prepared was a salmon mousse, and right before her party began, she caught her cat on the table, chowing down on the salmon. Angrily, she whisked the cat off the table and put it outside. What could she do with the salmon but smooth over the spot the cat had eaten? Just as she was finishing the body job on the salmon, the doorbell rang and the first of her guests arrived.

The party was tremendously successful and the woman hosting

the party felt like she'd finally been accepted into the high society of her town.

As the party was breaking up, she went to the back door to let her cat in. There, lying by the doorstep, was her cat, stone dead. Horrified, she called the town doctor and told him about the salmon mousse and poor kitty. Unfortunately, there was no choice, he told her. She had to announce what had happened to her guests, and they'd all have to go to the hospital to get their stomachs pumped.

She knew this was going to be the end of her social climbing days, but she thought it would be better to have angry guests than dead ones. So they formed a caravan, went to the hospital and, one by one, had their stomachs pumped. The hostess, humiliated, sat off in a corner of the waiting room and waited until the end to have the procedure. She avoided the gazes of her guests, and none of them spoke to her as they left the hospital. No one thanked her for a lovely evening.

She finally returned home at about 1:00 A.M., exhausted and demoralized. Strangely, her neighbor rushed out to greet her as her car pulled in the driveway. "Oh, it's awful. I'm so sorry," the neighbor said.

"Thank you," said the woman, searching her neighbor's face for any hint of sarcasm. After all, she hadn't been invited. But the woman seemed sincere.

"Yes, the whole evening was a disaster because of it," said the woman.

"I'm truly sorry," the neighbor said. "I know how much it must have meant to you."

"It meant the world," said the woman, thinking that no one would accept another party invitation from her as long as she lived.

"How long did you have it?" the neighbor asked.

"Oh, only about two hours, and then we found out and had to go to hospital."

The neighbor looked bewildered. "Well, I wish there was something I could have done. Your cat just ran behind the car as I was backing out of the driveway. And I was in such a rush that all I could do was place him by your back doorstep. When I returned home, I went over to explain, but you were gone. So I've been waiting for you ever since."

About two months after I heard the story and wrote it down in my journal, Mike Royko, a columnist for *The Chicago Tribune*, related the exact same story. Various people had told it to him, swearing it was true, that it had happened to a mother or a cousin or an aunt, and that it had taken place in Texas, Montreal or Baltimore. There are plenty of these cultural anecdotes floating around, and half of the people who tell them will swear they happened to someone they know.

An anecdote generally ends with a kind of punch line, the recognition by the reader or listener that something remarkable or laughable has happened. Contemporary stories demand a little more character development and sophistication than your average anecdote.

Character development, in fact, is the centerpiece of most short stories, and plot is secondary. Or rather, the plot should arise organically out of character development in a short story. As Janet Burroway says in her book *Writing Fiction* (HarperCollins), a character should want something and want it intensely. This desire or character motivation is the driving force in most short stories. The conflict arises from the character's desires being met or thwarted or ignored. Another way to put it is, *What does a character fear?* Or, *What does a character* not *want to happen?* Sometimes characters in a short story don't know what they want, and this can be part of the conflict as well. Or else they think they want one thing when they should want another. Or maybe they want a lot of things, too many things for one life to achieve. Grace Paley's story "Wants" in her collection *Enormous Changes at the Last Minute* (Farrar, Straus and Giroux) is a beautiful example of characters' desires coming into conflict. The story is barely more than three pages long, but Paley manages to write in such a richly textured way that the story seems completely realized in that short span. The story involves a woman who's returning a couple of Edith Wharton books to the public library. Sounds mundane enough, but the books are overdue by eighteen years. She meets, on the steps of the library, her ex-husband, and the two of them have a discussion, which at first seems harmless enough, but then devolves into acrimony, at least on the husband's part. He tells her he always wanted a sailboat and accuses her of never having wanted anything. This narrow and bitter remark leaves her stunned on the steps of the library. The rest of the story deals with her ruminations concerning what she wanted, things her insensitive husband could never guess.

So what about the anecdote about the salmon mousse? Isn't that a short story? After all, it contains most of the usual elements: conflict, crisis and resolution. The main character has a strong desire to better herself and is thwarted by the coincidence of her cat being run over by her neighbor.

Of all the anecdotes I've related so far, this one comes closest to being a story rather than an anecdote, partly because I doctored the anecdote (much as the unfortunate social climber doctored her salmon mousse), primarily by fleshing out the story, by inventing dialogue, and thus somewhat developing the character. The original anecdote, as I heard it, wouldn't take up more than a paragraph. Still, I'd say that the irony is too broad to make a successful short story. It relies too much on coincidence, on the punch line, to make it something more than a funny happening, something to relate at a party or to put in a newspaper column. Short stories usually go beneath the surface. That's not to say short stories should be dry and dull, but what happens should never be as important as to whom it happens. In an anecdote, *what* happens usually takes precedence over any serious character development.

There are basically three ways to use an anecdote in a short story. One way is to flesh out the anecdote, develop the characters and bring it beyond a simple punch line. I did this with a story called "Polish Luggage." It was based on an anecdote a woman told me about her father. He was an airline pilot who was incredibly racist and sexist and classist and other assorted "ists." He always complained that the "riff-raff" had taken to the skies ever since the airlines had started cutting their fares. He recognized "riff-raff" by their "Polish luggage." That's what he called shopping bags. He thought it was low-class to bring a shopping bag instead of a proper bag onto a plane.

For this and plenty of other reasons, the woman and her dad didn't get along. But when he died, all of their differences were forgotten, and she went home to his funeral.

The funeral was fairly elaborate. The mother had decided to have him cremated and then to have his ashes dropped from a plane to a hill on which she and her husband had watched the sunset on their first date.

When the family arrived at the little hangar, the funeral director took them to an office and explained what would happen when the plane was aloft. As he spoke, he opened a drawer, took out a shopping bag and dumped the father's ashes in it. The ashes had been in a beautiful urn, and when the daughter saw what was happening to her father, that he was taking his last journey in "Polish luggage," she was both horrified and amused.

The story was told to me on a Wisconsin farm owned by a couple of my friends from Chicago, and the woman who told me the story came over that day for that purpose. This might sound strange, but my hosts knew it was a good story, and the woman who told it wasn't a writer herself. (This wasn't the only story she told me on that day. I've got two more ideas based loosely on what she told me. And don't think I'm going to tell them to you. You might steal them.)

I loved the anecdote, but in writing the story, I obviously had to go beyond the punch line. The first order of business was deciding who the main character was going to be. I decided to keep the main character the daughter of the airline pilot, though I changed her character around a great deal. Not because of ethical considerations, in this case. I changed the character of the woman to make the material my own.

That's an important part of transforming real life (a phrase, by the way, I have trouble with. What's the alternative? Fake life?) into fiction. The way you claim ownership of a story is by using your imagination, by transforming the story into something new. If you don't, the events and characters of the story wind up owning you instead of the other way around. You'll be afraid to deviate from what really happened, and the story ultimately might suffer.

To give the story a little more flesh than the original anecdote, I decided to expand the mother's idea of dumping the father's ashes on the hill from which they viewed the sunset on their first date. I decided to turn the *whole* funeral into a reconcoction of the mother and father's first date. The narrator of the story naturally thinks her mother's a little kooky for coming up with such a plan, but she reluctantly goes along with it.

> The plan calls for a procession, stations of the cross fash-
> ion, from one memorable spot of their first date to an-

other. First, we'll drive past the Chinese restaurant where they had dinner that night, though it wasn't a Chinese restaurant then, but a fancy steak house with a seventeen-piece band. After that, we'll swing by the Parthenon Theater, and finally we'll trek out to the municipal airport where Daddy's ashes will be scattered from a plane high above the hill on which he and Mother watched the sunrise the next day. There's a dual beauty here, because Daddy was an airline pilot, though he would have preferred a 747 to a Cessna. Rather than being dropped, he would have liked the jet to explode him into Valhalla with his Viking ancestors.

Another way to use an anecdote, from your experience or someone else's, is to incorporate the anecdote as part of a story's dialogue, or make it a monologue. While an anecdote might not always work as the basis for an entire story, such an anecdote can work quite nicely as a way to show something about the personality of the character who's telling it. For instance, the anecdote of the man selling the pornographic key chains was something I decided to put in Angel's mouth as a way of further explicating her character, giving the reader an idea of what she considers important in life, what she thinks is right and wrong.

The third way to use an anecdote is to incorporate it into a story as one of several events, but not necessarily the main one. That's what I decided to do with the squirrel in the pizza box. The story in which that scene appears continues for another twelve pages. That way, although the anecdote still retains its punch line, it isn't the superficial culmination of the story.

ANECDOTES AND NOVELS

Novels, as well as stories, can evolve from anecdotes. Peter Turchi, the Director of the M.F.A. Program for Writers at Warren Wilson College, based his first novel, *The Girls Next Door* (New American Library), on an anecdote his father told him when he was young. "The story he told was this: In 1956 and again in early 1960, when my mother was pregnant with me, these people rented the house right next to theirs, and it became clear that they were running a whorehouse. But nobody ever saw them. These girls were never outside. My father had a station wagon and a U-Haul that he hooked up to it with demonstration models of industrial equipment that he was selling. And he would have to hook up the trailer to the station wagon every Monday morning before he went on his rounds. And he'd be gone for a few days.

"One time he backed up the station wagon and he didn't back it up quite far enough so he tried to lift up the hitch and pull the trailer forward, but of course it was too heavy for him. The three girls happened to be outside this one time, so they all came over and they gathered around him. And together they were able to pull it up to the car. He looked up at our kitchen window and there's my mother pregnant with me, and on either side of her, her parents glaring out at him. And that was it. That was the anecdote. That was his memory of these women. I think they left a couple of weeks after that. And he didn't know them by name, and didn't have any more interesting adventures with them."

Even though this anecdote became the basis for his novel, Turchi didn't immediately see it as such. At first, the novel had nothing to do with this story and was instead far afield from his own experience. Turchi's witty explanation of the evolution of his novel idea shows how novelists often roam far from their own imaginative territory, simply to arrive at material that's closer to home.

"I was in England for my junior year in college, and on one of the breaks I spent a couple of weeks in Paris in this fairly inexpensive hotel that was actually somebody's house in the Latin Quarter. A couple lived there with their boy who was eight or nine. Every morning I'd come down for breakfast and he'd be having his breakfast and doing his homework at the last minute. None of them spoke any English at all. And I spoke pretty poor French. I started to wonder what it would be like to grow up with your house as a hotel, kind of an Irving-esque idea, and seeing these strangers come through, not knowing what they're all about. And so I thought I would write this story or book about a boy who grew up in a family hotel in France. The problem was that I didn't know anything about Paris or France or anything about being a French boy. So I decided it might be a good idea to transport the whole notion for the story to Kansas, where this boy would grow up in a hotel. At least he'd be American. But of course, I'd never been to Kansas. I still don't know what made me think that would be a good place to set a novel. It should come as no surprise that I finally decided to set the story in Baltimore, the only place I'd lived of those three.

"Then I started thinking maybe it shouldn't be the boy's story because that's already kind of a cliché, the coming-of-age novel. Then I thought maybe it would be the story told by one of the boarders in the house, somebody who lived there regularly and watched this family, which is sort of the position I'd been in. And then he was going to watch something going on across the street. And finally, it turned out not to be the boy or a boarder, but the father. Somehow I realized in there that the story had grown awfully close to the story that I remembered my father telling.

"For whatever reason, my first impulse was not to find out anything more about what really happened. In fact, I found out everything I know now about what happened in 1960, beyond what I've just related, after the novel was published. All sorts of people from the neighborhood came up to me to tell me their tales about these prostitutes, which were great. It would have been wonderful material—for a different book."

Turchi's hunch that he should rely on his own imagination rather than the real events of that time was undoubtedly the wisest choice to make. While the real material might have added a different dimension to the novel, it also might have bogged him down, or made him feel too responsible to the way things actually happened rather than the way they needed to happen in the novel. By reimagining events, he was able to make the material his own and divorce himself from pure remembrance. "I kept trying to imagine what it must have felt like to be my father back then, and in fact, the first draft of the novel included his occupation. Probably the only reason the novel is set in 1960 is because I was working from that anecdote. And it was probably pretty heavily flavored by the innocence with which he told the anecdote.

"What became important to me finally in writing the novel was not the premise but what the main character was understanding in terms of his family. The real job of putting that novel together was trying to incorporate that rich anecdote into what I finally became much more interested in exploring in terms of character. That shuffling together, that integration, took seven years to figure out."

STORIES VERSUS NOVELS

Whether you write a novel or a short story depends largely on your material and what kind of writer you are. Stories are much more like poems than they are like novels. Stories tend to be as tightly constructed as poems and are generally much more concerned with an economical use of language than novels are. In a story, a character might be described by a gesture; in a novel, by three or four pages of description and flashback. Digressions are much more possible in novels than in short stories. A scene that might make a nice side trip in a novel will most likely seem utterly unnecessary in a story if it doesn't directly relate to the main character. In a novel, different points of view can be more easily explored, while they might seem jarring in a short story. Although figurative language (metaphors, similes) is used by both novelists and short story writers, a good short story writer can create a jewel of a central metaphor so sharp and fine you'll marvel at the craft. No one says you must stick to one form or the other, though often writers, like Flannery O'Connor, will excel in short stories but not novels—or vice versa.

A friend once told me that he found it so difficult to create a believable character whom the reader cared about that he wouldn't let that character go after one short story. If that's how you feel about your characters, you're probably best suited for the novel form. If, however, you find yourself fascinated by the moment, by brief flashes of life, the short story might be your form.

One cautionary note, however. Writing workshops are best suited for the discussion and dissection of short stories, not novels. While some noble teachers attempt novel writing workshops, the workshops could be harmful if not handled correctly. Novels are fragile things, and many fledgling novels have been nipped in the bud by a writing workshop. If you turn in the first thirty pages of your novel before you've written the next three hundred, your peers will inevitably treat it like a short story. What might seem like a fault in a short story (uncertainty about the direction of the story, lack of closure, unexplained happenings) can hardly be avoided in the beginning of a novel. Maybe your peers can praise the quality of your writing, but they can't give you direction. You're the one with the overall conception of the novel. Your classmates are clueless. A novel cannot be written by committee — so don't attempt it. The other pitfall of this approach is "first chapter-itis," rewriting your first chapter over and over again to your classmates' delight but your own frustration. What you'll wind up with is a perfect first chapter with closure, direction and explained happenings — in other words, a short story!

Exercises

1. Write an anecdote, something someone told you or that you observed. This should be a story you're quite familiar with, something that you've told before. Write the opening scene of the anecdote, a page or two, then make notes on how you would transform it into a story, how you would go beyond the punch line. Who is the main character? What does that character want or fear?

2. Using the same anecdote, create a character who tells another character this tale. Describe the setting and circumstances in which this character relates the anecdote. Pay special attention to the reactions of the character being told the anecdote, and also what the telling of the anecdote shows about the speaker's personality.

3. Take a family incident from your childhood and write it exactly as you remember it, without embellishment. After you've finished, ask a relative how he or she remembers this incident. Are there any major or even minor differences in the way he or she remembers the event? Why do you think this is?

4. Use this same memory as the basis of a fictional scene, using a combination of dialogue, action, description, thoughts and exposition. What choices will you have to make to fictionalize it? Are there details or characters you have to add or leave out in the fictional treatment?

5. Write this same scene over again from a point of view not your own. How have the details changed? How has the memory changed?

CHAPTER THREE

Focusing
Real Life

You now have some idea of the various forms, but another question must be answered: How do we impose order on something as messy as real life? Order, after all, is the essential difference between real life and fiction. Real life, if yours is anything like mine, tends toward chaos. Fiction has structure, order, refinement. Imposing the artificial — that's what fiction writers do to turn their stories into art. Fiction can be boisterous, even obnoxious at times. The art of writing fiction, like a good magic trick, is often in making it seem easy, effortless — in never letting the reader see all the practice you've put into it.

The temptation, which must always be resisted, is to include *everything* that happened, rather than making wise selections. Be parsimonious with your experience. Don't give it added weight simply because you're fond of the memory. If you include everything that happened, your book or story risks becoming muddled and weighted down by a voluminous chronicle of your associations. Remember, this is a piece of fiction, not a slide show of your various experiences. If you let the structure of your story or novel collapse, the reader will stop paying attention to what you've written.

Every novel or short story has a *handle* — that is, something the writer and reader can grab onto, a reference point, something that makes us feel like we're in good hands with someone who knows where he is headed. Anything can be a handle. What we're ultimately after is *focus*. Your handle is simply your focusing element.

Novelist Elly Welt even took the concept literally. When she was working on her novel *Berlin Wild* (Viking), her husband brought her a wooden handle he'd found while walking on the beach. She hung it on the wall above her writing desk. And that was what she looked at for inspiration when she was writing.

The following are some handles to help you rein in your life and tame it to the world of fiction. These can be used for either stories or novels, and none of these forms, of course, is restricted to stories that are based on real life. In succeeding chapters, we'll discuss various types of stories that come from real life, but for now it might be good to have some basic ideas of the ways in which authors structure their works of fiction.

FOCUSING ON A CHARACTER

In *Making Shapely Fiction* (Norton), Jerome Stern defines voice as: "the writer's style as it is expressed in the character's speech and thoughts." Point of view is basically the central consciousness of the story (or chapter from a novel, as the case may be). It might seem like the simplest choice, when writing about a real event, to write from the point of view based on your own. But often, the character based on yourself is really unnecessary, and any time you have a character who isn't important to the story, you should cut her out. Writers tend to be observers. Even though we write about people in conflict, we tend to stay out of the fray ourselves, preferring instead a comfortable seat from the sidelines. The Hemingways are much rarer than the Prousts; rather than big-game hunters, writers are more often slightly hypochondriacal, neurotic imaginers who lock themselves in their rooms all day.

So, often when we write a story, whether based on real life or not, we'll include a passive narrator who has no role in the story other than serving as the reader's eyes and ears. Sometimes this works. A famous example is Nick in *The Great Gatsby*, but more often than not, the passive narrator simply gets in the way. If, however, you feel that a character based on yourself must be the narrator, make sure that he plays some active role, that the events of the story affect him in some way. (Don't misunderstand me. I'm not saying that Nick was based on Fitzgerald himself. Fitzgerald was undoubtedly more like Gatsby than Nick. Maybe that's why both characters worked so well. Fitzgerald was able to create enough distance to fashion a character *unlike* himself, viewing a character *like* himself.)

Often, the worst strategy for writing a story is to have one character telling another character or characters the story of her life. It's a rather bald device, used to good effect by Joseph Conrad and others in earlier days, but a little too familiar to capture most readers' attention these days. Of course, if you can twist this idea around and make it fresh, you might succeed.

It's usually best to cut out the listener and tell the story from the point of view of one of the principals. You also must decide whether you will write the story in first or third person or, less frequently, second person. Delmore Schwartz uses second person in "In Dreams Begin Responsibilities," his haunting story about a young man dreaming that he's watching a film of his parents on their first date. We can't assume, of course, that it's actually based on a true account of his parents' meeting. The writer always has the defense (sometimes more accurate than at other times) that there is a difference between the author and the narrator of a story. Ideally, you want every story you write to seem autobiographical, to seem authentic in its emotions as well as its physical details, so that the reader is tricked into thinking "this really happened."

First person is useful in letting a character speak for himself. In a first-person story, the distance between the reader and the character's psyche, what John Gardner calls "psychic distance," is foreshortened. And since we tend as listeners to more readily believe something told *by* someone than *about* someone, first person can often lend an aura of authenticity.

If you still are unsure of what voice is, listen to this opening of Barry Hannah's story "Water Liars":

> When I am run down and flocked around by the world, I go down to Farte Cove off the Yazoo River and take my beer to the end of the pier where the old liars are still snapping and wheezing at one another. The line-up is always different, because they're always dying out or succumbing to constipation, etc., whereupon they go back to the cabins and wait for a good day when they can come out and lie again, leaning on the rail with coats full of bran cookies. The son of the man the cove was named for is often out there. He pronounces his name Far*tay*, with a great French stress on the last syllable. Otherwise

you might laugh at his history or ignore it in favor of the name as it's spelled on the sign.

I'm glad it's not my name.

Don't use first person simply to get closer to a character. In third person, limited, you can get just as close to a character as with first. You also shouldn't write in first person simply because the story happened to you. In that case, you might be better off writing in third person so you can transform the story into a fictional realm. And voice isn't necessarily more prominent in first than third person, though it often is. But listen to the opening paragraph of Marjorie Sandor's story, "Victrola." The voice here is as different as can be from Barry Hannah's, but it's no less sure and strong. We still have a definite sense of the way the character thinks and speaks, though the story is told in third person. We also have the overlying consciousness of the narrator, who directs us through the child's world:

> She was stubborn from day one. For her, words like fate or destiny, words we throw around, were as real as the roots of the live oak, spreading under the sidewalk where no one can see them but the child who stands directly under the tree, imagination intact. She didn't know what life intended for her, but it was obvious to the casual observer that she meant to have one, since she eluded death and disaster so well, even when her mother, the beautiful idiot, was managing things. By the time Francisca was eight years old, she had already survived three Mazatlan epidemics and the stings of two deadly scorpions. She was also known for her tendency to have fever dreams that nobody could decipher. It was just after the second scorpion and its accompanying dream that she awoke to see her father's yellow guitar sailing through the air across their shed.

The point of view you choose will naturally mold your story and keep it from being too messy. When you change point of view, you change the story. Experiment. Explore your options. If a story based on a real event doesn't work from one point of view, try another.

FOCUSING ON A SETTING

Sometimes the setting of your story or novel can be the handle you're looking for. Think of how Tara, the antebellum southern estate, functions in *Gone With the Wind*. It's the driving force behind most of Scarlett's actions. It's her motivation for most of what she does. When all else is crumbling around her, she still believes in her land. Other writers have used setting as the organizing principle behind a collection of stories: James Joyce's *Dubliners* and Sherwood Anderson's *Winesburg, Ohio* immediately leap to mind.

The writer Steve Yarbrough uses his hometown of Indianola, Mississippi, as his organizing principle. All the stories in his collection *Family Men* (Louisiana State University Press) are centered in or around Indianola, and this gives the book a kind of unity, much the way a novel has a sense of cohesiveness.

FOCUSING ON THE STORY

At some point in a novel or a short story, the reader needs a sense of direction. Some readers will give a novel a hundred pages to get going, some will allow only fifty, but if you ramble from one episode to another, your reader might not stick with you for long at all. An episode is an event within a series of events. If these events do not seem connected by a cause/effect relationship, we say the story or novel seems episodic or rambling. Short stories are sometimes criticized for being too episodic — there's no thread pulling the reader along. Sometimes episodic stories can work as long as something else holds the story together, such as a theme or a strong voice.

Scenes are the same as episodes, except they're more purposeful. Scenes are constructed. Episodes just happen. Our memories tend to be episodic. We remember in associative flashes. A scene is an episode consciously molded into the confines of a story. When we speak of a scene in a movie, a novel or a play, we talk about an episode confined to one time and place. If the time or place shifts, we've gone on to a new scene.

We remember the time our older brother tied a string to one of our back molars and tried to yank it out by tying the other end of the string to the bathroom door and slamming it. Maybe that memory leads to another episode: our older brother lining our G.I. Joes against the wall of our house and blowing them apart with his BB gun. Now we remember how every Sunday morning our brother woke us up at six and forced us to help deliver the bulky Sunday edition of the paper. For this, he paid us a nickel or half a candy bar — our choice.

All these events happened at different times in our lives. The tooth-pulling incident took place when we were five. The BB gun execution took place when we were nine. The paper route exploitation took place when we were seven. No problem, as far as that's concerned. For the purposes of fiction, you can always collapse events together. No one but your mother and your older brother will care that these events didn't happen at the same time. Remember, you're writing a story, not a family history.

But let's further examine these events. How are they connected? They all show certain aspects of sibling rivalry, an older brother bullying a younger one. Are we leaving anything out? Of course. We're almost certainly leaving out the fact that the younger brother was no angel either, and that he probably tormented his older brother, too — though how he did this escapes us at the moment.

So will this make a good basis for a story? Not in its present form. Right now, it's just three episodes, all of which make the same point about the brothers and their relationship. It's true that sometimes you want to repeat themes in your writing, to reinforce them in your reader's mind, but episodes should not seem repetitive; they should build, one upon the other, to enlarge our understanding of the characters in the story.

BRAINSTORMING

To fit these autobiographical episodes into a story or a novel, we must enlarge the story first. A simple story about two brothers who don't get along might make a good anecdote, but it's nothing new. What's the angle? What's the spin? What makes this story different from all other stories about sibling rivalry? What makes it unique?

When I'm stuck like this, I brainstorm — that is, I think of more associations from my life. I write them in my journal. I make notes. Eventually, I find the story.

Okay, these episodes occurred between my older brother and me in the sixties when we were growing up. Is there anything else

I remember about him and our relationship from that time? There was the time his friend from New York, Danny, came to visit us in Athens, Ohio, where we'd moved from New York. He and Danny decided to build a bomb. I wanted to build a bomb with them, but they told me I was too young. So they went off on their own and I stayed home and built my own bomb, starting with a Windex bottle and pouring everything I could imagine from under the sink into it. Then I found some matches in one of my father's jackets and went into the field behind our house and lit the shoelace fuse which I'd soaked in Windex. Flames shot out of the bottle, and the field near our house caught fire. I remember how surprised I was, not that I thought it wouldn't work, but I wasn't prepared for the consequences. I was in my tennis shoes and I began stamping the flames furiously. Somehow, I managed to get them all out, though my tennis shoes melted in the process and my feet were burned.

Good episode, but still an episode. I think we're getting closer, but we still haven't found the glue to hold these episodes together.

Okay, another episode. The memory of my mother and father fighting and how my older brother, sister (who was eighteen and old enough at the time to buy alcohol) and I walked into town and she bought them a bottle of champagne so they'd stop. I think it worked. I remember feeling special as I walked into town with my older siblings—how we were acting as a kind of united front.

Now we're getting close to seeing this as a whole story and not as a series of episodes. The key is that we've started getting close to the feelings of the characters, rather than simply reporting events. It is who the characters are—what motivates them, what makes them change—that are the crucial elements of fiction, not the events themselves. That idea or theme of consequences—of children not knowing the consequences of their actions and adults not caring sometimes about the consequences of their actions—appeals to me, as does the feeling I had of acting in unity with my brother and sister.

The sister here, for the purposes of our story, probably isn't necessary, so let's get rid of her. I like the idea of making bombs. It seems unique, a new spin on sibling rivalry: competing bomb factories! We probably should keep the time frame the sixties, which, after all, was a good time for making bombs. And what enlarges the story beyond the sibling rivalry? The conflict between the parents. The two conflicts will be parallel in our story.

As I said, I like the idea of consequences—the consequences of both adult actions and the actions of children. Now let's decide whose point of view the story should be in. We've got the choice of an older brother, say, about thirteen; a younger brother, eight; and the parents. Each would tell a different story.

I would choose the older brother for several reasons. By taking the story out of my own experience, I would give my imagination more freedom and I wouldn't feel compelled to record my experiences as they really happened. It might also give me a better insight into my older brother. I also like the in-between age of thirteen— one foot in childhood, the other in adulthood.

BLOCKING SCENES

But we still need to focus. One way to do this is to block the scenes— write notes on the various scenes as you envision them, before you begin writing the story. This process can be frustrating and time consuming, but it's one of the best ways to clear your head and find some focus to your material.

The scenes won't necessarily stay the same as you conceive of them. Your conception of a story almost always changes as you get farther into it, and you must allow this to happen. Don't try to force your story in one direction simply because that's the way you originally envisioned it. With Peter Turchi's novel *The Girls Next Door*, his dilemma was to figure out how to take the initial anecdote of his family living next door to a house of prostitution and transform an essentially passive, voyeuristic story into one in which characters were interacting.

"There are some important differences between the appeal of an anecdote and the necessary complexity of a novel," Turchi says. "For one thing, I realized it wouldn't be enough for this character to simply observe these people from the distance of the driveway for 250 pages. There was going to have to be some real interaction. So I tried to imagine the various relationships this person could have with those people and at the same time maintain a certain curious distance. Almost all of the scenes are fabricated. Novelist and short story writer Ron Hansen gave me some advice at the Bread Loaf Writers Conference. I had a character who was interested in baseball because the whole time I was growing up in Baltimore, the Orioles were often in the World Series. The character was also fascinated by these characters across the driveway. So Hansen told me these prostitutes have got to play baseball. My first response was 'What a ludicrous suggestion,' but I went home and in the next month wrote a scene in which the prostitutes have a softball game and a picnic. It worked. What it really showed me was that the premise had to be set in motion. It wasn't enough to have the possibility of something interesting happen, but it had to start paying off in different ways. Sometimes it's tempting to try to avoid the greatest confrontations. I still think it's good advice to try to discover the most obvious, the most dramatic confrontation and seeing if it will work."

So let's look for the most dramatic possibilities in our hypothetical story. One other point before we block it out and try to make our discoveries: Often the final image of my story will pop into my head before I've started to write the story. I might not even know what the image means. And that's fine. As I told you earlier, fiction is a discovery process. You don't necessarily know everything about your characters when you begin to write your story. You learn about them as you go along. In this case, I see the field on fire and the younger brother surrounded by flames, trying vainly to put them out.

Fire and bombs. We've come a long way from simple sibling rivalry. Something is pretty wrong with this family. What is it? Remember, stories involve conflict, and even though the story might be modeled on your family members, you may have to change them for the sake of the story in ways that make you uncomfortable. But, at this point you need to be careful. Simply overlaying a larger, more powerful conflict on your story could ring a little false—say, if you make the real conflict in the story incest or divorce. If you're not careful, the subject might overwhelm the story and the reader might feel like she has stepped into a talk show rather than a short story. Let's stick with this theme of family warfare and see where it leads.

There are a couple of other facts I've held back from you. (When you find yourself doing that, you know those are the ones you shouldn't hold back. What's most powerful is often what you most want to hide.)

First, I was definitely my mother's favorite, and my older brother was my father's. This wasn't any big secret in our family. My father accused my mother of spoiling me, and he was right. My mother always took my side in a fight with my brother, and my father always took my brother's side. The year I was eight and my brother was thirteen, my father died. Of course, that changed the family dynamics forever. Also, my brother lost his ally.

Now I think we're getting somewhere. This seems to me to be the central conflict and a way to unify all the disparate episodes — how they all relate to warfare and how my father was the first casualty. Part of learning how to write autobiographical fiction is learning how to dig deeper and deeper, to try to understand why a particular event or time stands out for you — and it's not always for the reasons you think.

Here are some notes I wrote just now:

Bombs — central image

Bottles — champagne bottle, Windex bottle.

These bottle images are something I'll probably keep in mind throughout the story. Maybe the beginning of a central metaphor. Now I see a definite thread here.

Scene One — I'd probably start the story with the older brother blowing up the younger brother's G.I. Joes, maybe getting yelled at by his mother, and establishing the fact that the father has died. The older brother expects a visit from a friend from the good old days when they lived in New York. Maybe here I'd also introduce the bottle of champagne. One of the brothers has saved it because he likes the bottle.

Scene Two — Maybe the next scene would show some kind of retaliation on the younger brother's part. The mother, predictably, takes the younger brother's side, perhaps even subtly or not so subtly blames the older brother for his father's death. The older brother plans revenge or running away; secretly he calls his best friend from New York. The next day, the two brothers deliver papers together in relative calm. The younger brother, being young and dumb, doesn't realize that payment of half a candy bar or a nickel is not a very good deal.

Scene Three — Danny's visit. Bombs.

Note how sketchy those notes are, especially the last ones. Not having written the story yet, I can't know precisely where it will lead, nor all the connections and revelations I will make along the way. Right now, I want to play around with the idea of destruction and the various conflicts, both external and internal. I wonder, for instance, if the older brother believes he killed his father, and I wonder how self-destructive his actions are.

The story might work. It might not. If I've done my job right and have some idea of cause/effect and understand the relationships among the various characters, my story will fit together into a series of unified scenes. If not, the story will seem episodic. That's the risk you take any time you set down to work on a story or novel. Not every story works, especially those created from the hash of memory. But at least I have some direction now.

TIME FRAMES

One of the most common ways to impose a structure on your story or novel is through a *time frame*. Louisa May Alcott did this with *Little Women* (Scholastic Inc.). The story was semiautobiographical, based on her childhood in the 1840s. The character of Jo was modeled on her. But Alcott structured her story by making everything happen in a year. She also changed the time, setting the story in the 1860s rather than the 1840s. Alcott's real father, Bronson Alcott, was a complex man, one of the leaders of the transcendentalists. Instead of dealing with his character, Alcott got rid of him. She sent him off to war.

You can choose whatever time frame you want. There are short stories that take place over a year or a lifetime, and there are novels that cover only one day, but the novel is really the medium for exploring the effects of time on a character or situation. And short stories generally deal with briefer time spans — one moment, one situation and its effects. There are no hard-and-fast rules about this. These are just tendencies of the forms. Some writers like to play around with time, stretching it as far as it can go. Nicholson Baker's novel *The Mezzanine* (Weidenfeld and Nicolson) takes place in a thirty-second escalator ride. James Joyce's novel *Ulysses* takes place in one day. Back in Shakespeare's time, the convention was that a play's time frame could not exceed twenty-four hours. Shakespeare was considered a radical for breaking with this tradition.

FOCUSING ON METAPHOR, SYMBOL OR THEME

Another strategy for reining in your novel or short story is to weave in a central metaphor. An example of an autobiographical novel with a central metaphor is *The Bell Jar* by Sylvia Plath. Another is the play *The Glass Menagerie* by Tennessee Williams. Laura's menagerie functions beautifully as a metaphor of the girl's own fragility, just as the bell jar functions as a symbol of Plath's claustrophobia.

A metaphor should come organically from the story itself; it should never simply be inserted into a story. Writers, good writers, don't say, "I think I need a bird metaphor in this here story." By consciously inserting a metaphor into a story, you will probably wind up with a metaphor that's been used time and again, to the point of being a cliché. And your metaphor will seem obvious if it's simply inserted here and there.

By "organic," I mean that the metaphor should not be forced but should arise naturally from the characters or situation. The trick is to trust your intuition, at least during the first draft. If your character says, "He wants me to be a goddess and I want to be Mickey Mouse," see where that image leads. Develop it. Echo it later in the story. Have it crop up in a different context. *You don't always need to know what a phrase or a gesture or a description* means *as you're writing it.* Trust your unconscious. Writing is a discovery process, and part of the fun of writing is learning why you just wrote what you did.

Perhaps that sounds outlandish to some, but it's the way most writers work. Flannery O'Connor started her story "Good Country People" with a dialogue between two women based on O'Connor's mother and a neighbor. Halfway down the page, O'Connor gave the first woman a daughter. Then she decided to give the daughter a wooden leg. She didn't know why she had a wooden leg or what it would mean, but she allowed the image to develop. And by the end of the story, the wooden leg functions beautifully as an organic symbol, if not a central metaphor. A bible salesman, who turns out to be a con artist, winds up stealing the wooden leg from the daughter, who up to that point has considered herself too intelligent and worldly to be taken in by anyone—especially by this salesman, whom she considers to be just another country bumpkin. In synopsis, the story sounds outlandish, and it is, in a brilliant way. Still, it works, and by the end of this story you believe that this bible salesman would indeed have a thing for the daughter's wooden leg and want to make off with it.

That's the idea of *symmetry* again. A good writer doesn't abandon an image or idea but sees where it will lead. Nothing happens for no good reason. If your character has a wooden leg because you want her to, but nothing is made of the leg in the story, take it out. If it doesn't serve a purpose, it doesn't belong.

A theme is the central idea of the story or novel. Often, there's more than one theme, and the themes are interconnected. Writers sometimes organize their work around a particular theme. In "Good Country People," such a theme is the difference between *professing* to be good or intelligent, and actually *being* good or intelligent. The trick is to avoid letting your theme overwhelm your characters. Don't have your characters act in a certain way simply because it fits your theme, rounds out your metaphor or shows what a brilliant symbolist you are. There's nothing worse than pretentious prose full of symbols, themes and metaphors galore, but little in the way of believable characters.

JOURNEYS

The oldest form in fiction, according to Jerome Stern in *Making Shapely Fiction*, is the *journey*. A journey has a natural structure to it. There's the beginning, and then there's the end. One of my favorite journey stories, and one of the oldest, is the story of Jonah. This is really a short short story, almost minimalist, about the prophet Jonah's foolhardy attempts to go against God's will. It has all the elements of any good short story: conflict, character motivation and revelation. Jonah, a prophet, is commanded by God to go to Nineveh and preach to the city's inhabitants so they may be saved. But Jonah, who considers the people of Nineveh his enemy, doesn't want them to be saved, so he runs in the other direction, sets out to sea, gets caught in a storm, is thrown overboard and is swallowed by a whale. Finally, he gets the message. "If I'd known it meant that much to you . . ." he tells God, or something to that effect, and he finally sets out for Nineveh. He preaches to the inhabitants and, lo and behold, they all repent, and the city is saved. Everyone is joyous except for Jonah, who goes outside the city gates, sits beneath the shade of a gourd and thinks black thoughts. God, seeing this, decides to make the gourd wither and die. That's the last straw for Jonah, who gets up and asks God why he had to go and do such a low-down thing as taking away his shade. This is the climax of the story, the point at which things change—and a story inevitably involves change. God basically says, "Look, you didn't create this gourd. And you didn't create the city of Nineveh. I did, so it's only for me to decide what lives and what dies." The story ends on an anticlimactic note: "And should not I pity Nineveh, that great city in which there are more than a hundred and twenty thousand persons who do not know their right hand from their left, and also much cattle?" Cattle? Kind of undercuts the story's power.

Some of the great classics of American literature have been journey stories. In *As I Lay Dying*, Faulkner chronicles one family's journey to bury its mother. In *The Grapes of Wrath*, Steinbeck depicts the Joads in their struggle to reach the promised land of California from their dustbowl home in Depression-era Oklahoma. In all of these journeys there's plenty of conflict, plenty of roadblocks thrown in the way of the characters on their journeys. And the roadblocks aren't only physical, but spiritual and emotional as well. By the end of these journeys, we know and deeply care about the fates of these characters.

THE BIG EVENT

A good way to organize a story or a novel is to structure it within an event: a game, a hunt, a wedding, a funeral. But you need to be careful with this form. Stay away from stasis, or lack of movement. Try to push the boundaries of whatever activity you've chosen to write about. If your characters are attending a wedding or funeral, try to see this event in a new light. Don't fall back on the standard clichés that surround such an event.

Almost everyone tries out one of these stories at some point or another. But they usually begin something like this:

> Grandma Pickins wasn't the best woman in the world, thought Jolene, sitting by herself in the front row of the Thunderbolt Baptist Church in Floyd's Knobs, Mississippi. But she wasn't the worst woman in the world, neither. Suddenly, her reverie was broken by the sight of Mabel Lee Mopes, her head bowed reverently in the opposite pew. Why that hussy, thought Jolene. How dare she show her face in here. Soon, Jolene was lost in reverie again . . .

And so on, until the reader loses himself or herself in reverie, too, and decides to go on to something more fun to do.

Jerome Stern calls this type of story, in which the main action is confined to a small space, a "bathtub story." In *Making Shapely Fiction* he writes, "While in that space the character thinks, remembers, worries, plans, whatever. Before long, readers realize that the character is not going to do anything."

I once read a story collection in which the characters kept falling asleep. In each story, page after page would be devoted to a central character getting drowsy, nodding off, and slowly losing consciousness. The book had the same effect on me.

Of course, you can successfully turn around such an event as a wedding and make it lively and new. If you recall my story from chapter two, "Polish Luggage," I ignored my own advice and wrote about a funeral. There's no subject matter that's taboo. It's a matter of casting the subject in new light. But certain stories are notorious among creative writing teachers, "dead grandmother stories" being at the top of the list.

Games can be great organizers for stories, too. One of the best I know of is Charles Dickinson's story, "Risk," based on the board game of world conquest. Dickinson's story is a tour de force in which he juggles the points of view of a group of friends who meet regularly to play this game. If you've ever played Risk, you'll remember how brutal it can be—almost as bad as croquet. But, as in any good story, the real conflict is beneath the surface, in the characters' secret lives that they reveal to the reader, but not to one another as each tries to take over the world. The game, as well as its name and all that the word *risk* implies, becomes a central metaphor of the organic variety we previously discussed. Here is the story's second paragraph:

> Frank is the first to arrive. Then Nolan. Frank wore dirty clothes that afternoon when he took the laundry down to the big machines in the basement of his apartment building; with the load in the washer, soap measured, and coins slotted, he added the clothes he was wearing and made the long walk back upstairs to his apartment naked. He paused to read the fine print on the fire extinguisher. Noises in the building set birds loose in his heart. Frank takes the red armies when they gather to play the game of world conquest.

What's especially remarkable about this story is the way in which Dickinson takes a static event like playing a board game and makes it seem anything but static. You can do the same with a game of chess, checkers, mah-jongg, croquet, marbles, whatever. The trick is to know your characters and their internal conflicts. Whether the conflict spills over into the orderliness of the game or remains internalized but reflected in the game is up to you.

A fishing expedition or a hunt can be a good focus for a story as well. Think of Hemingway's "The Short Happy Life of Francis Macomber" or Norman Maclean's *A River Runs Through It* (University of Chicago Press) or Faulkner's "The Bear" from *Go Down Moses*. But what you need to keep in mind, especially if you base your hunting story on a real-life experience (or any other stories based on real-life events), is that a lot of other people have been through these experiences before. You're not the first person who's used a deer hunt as the basis for a coming-of-age story. You're not the first person who's noticed that people can be hypocritical at funerals and weddings. You don't want your story to seem clichéd and boring. You want it to seem original and lively, much like the Charles Dickinson paragraph above. The trick is in making your characters seem real, and one of the best ways to do that is to base them, at least in part, on real people you've known or observed — which is something we'll discuss in the next chapter.

Exercises

1. We've all been to carnivals and fairs. Write a memory of a fair or carnival in as much detail as you can. Now make that the setting for the opening of a short story. But don't base the main character on yourself. If other memories of other carnivals flood in, be sure to include them.

2. Think about someone you've known well, someone from your family perhaps: a brother, sister, mother, father. First, write as many memories and associations of this person as possible. Mark the memories that seem especially resonant to you—ones that seem either most moving or that best show the personality of your subject. Now, brainstorm a bit and cast these memories in a fictional context. Block out scenes. Make associations. Write an outline for a story based on these memories. Be sure to stay focused.

3. Go somewhere with your journal and observe some people. Go to a mall, a park, a grocery store. Write down a description of these people. Now introduce a character in conflict with these people or a character who in some ways gets involved with these people—much as Peter Turchi got his prostitutes playing softball.

4. Organize the opening of a story around a game that you remember playing or observing someone else play: your grandmother playing Twister, you playing Scrabble, your younger brother playing croquet. Explore the relationships of your characters as they play this game.

5. Base a short short story of no more than a thousand words on a memory. Organize the story around a time frame: a day, a year, an hour, a minute. You may, if you want, use some of the ready-made structures we've discussed above: a game, a journey. A time frame or a central metaphor might emerge in relation to

your characters. You'll notice that some memories will fit your imposed structure and some won't. Jettison the ones that don't fit, and mold your memories to fit your structure. It's more important for the story to work than for the memories to be accurate.

CHAPTER FOUR

Real People

We rarely write about other people simply as they're presented to us, mostly because we don't know all the facts of their lives and so we have to make some of them up. There's nothing wrong with that. In many cases, knowing too little about someone is preferable to knowing too much. If you write a story based on a family member, for instance, or a friend, your feelings of affection and friendship for that person can easily get in the way of your story or novel. In other words, you'll leave things out—maybe the best parts of the story, maybe the details that intrigued you about this person in the first place—to protect your friend's privacy. That might be the ethical thing to do—an issue we'll explore more in depth in a later chapter—but it might also kill your story.

TRANSFORMATIONS

Usually, there's a middle ground between imagining a character whole cloth and writing something completely biographical about someone you know. You must remember that you're writing fiction, not biography. Fiction, by its nature, involves transformation. If you want to write about Uncle Lou, go ahead, but don't make him Uncle Lou. First of all, think about what makes him so intriguing to you. That central ingredient, of course, is what you'll most likely want to keep. Let's say Uncle Lou believes in ghosts. This is something that's always fascinated you about him. This belief in ghosts sprang from an early childhood experience, when Uncle Lou was allegedly visited in the middle of the night by the ghost of his father. Other than this belief in ghosts, Uncle Lou seems rather plain and unexceptional to you. He's a balding, overweight bachelor. His politics are on the conservative side. He's a quiet man who eats dinner every night with his widowed sister, your Aunt Elena — she does all the cooking and cleaning. While she's in the kitchen fixing dinner, he's out in the living room reading *The Wall Street Journal*. During dinner, he hardly talks to Aunt Elena, and afterward, he departs with hardly a word.

Now you have two characters from your life, and this somewhat strange relationship between them — the kernel of a story. And what about Aunt Elena? Does she believe in ghosts, too? Or does she think Uncle Lou is just a little daffy?

Obviously, there are problems here if you want to write about these people. You may be a little reluctant to change too much about the characters and the situation. At the same time, you don't want to offend Aunt Elena or Uncle Lou. You don't want them to be able to recognize themselves. So you have two choices. Either you can wait until your uncle and aunt pass away to write about them, or you can change them. You can change their ages. But no, what interests you about them is that they're both older, a little lonely, a little dependent on each other, and also obsessed with something that might or might not have occurred when Lou was a little boy: the sighting of his dead father. Okay, so change their sexes. Make Aunt Elena the one who saw the ghost. Do they have to be brother and sister? How about husband and wife? Must it be their dead father? What about their mother or a stranger? Can you change the outward appearance of Uncle Lou? Depicting him as balding might offend him more than the way you portray his belief in ghosts. That's what happened to a friend of mine who wrote of a mutual friend in a story. He was cast as a short-order cook, a complete fabrication, but in every other way my friend captured his personality perfectly, from his wise-cracking sense of humor to his receding hairline. The mention of the receding hairline was, of course, what upset him.

The fact is, you can rarely tell what will or won't offend someone in a story you've written about them. The best you can do is to change whatever you can bear to change about them. Make your Uncle Lou a short-order cook. Make Aunt Elena the owner of the diner. Or change the locale. Above all, don't mess with male pattern baldness.

All of this is done not simply to protect Uncle Lou and Aunt Elena's privacy, but for your sake as well. In a way, you must stop thinking of them as your real-life relatives for the story to be successful. You must cut loose from your ties to these people or else your story will seem stilted and you'll be afraid to take risks. The more you transform these people into combinations of your imagination and who they really are, the more liberated you'll feel in writing your story. Remember, just because you *base* a character on Aunt Elena doesn't mean you're restricted to the facts.

Mixing and Matching

Another way to transform your characters is by making them into *composites* — that is, a mix of your Uncle Lou and perhaps other real people you know, people who have a certain Lou-ness about them. This way, Uncle Lou will not simply be Uncle Lou, but also perhaps your friend's father, and maybe a pinch of some stranger you once saw in passing and wrote about in your journal. By making a composite character, you actually enrich the character. Real observed detail only enhances a story.

David Michael Kaplan used a composite character in "Anne Rey," a story about an art restorer who goes to live on a sailboat and whose mother is suffering from a mysterious brain ailment. The whole seed idea for "Anne Rey" came from seeing a license plate.

"I was driving along on an L.A. freeway," Kaplan says. "A car passed me and the license plate says Anne Ray. That intrigued me and I wrote it down in my journal, which I had in my car. Just Anne Ray. I changed it to Rey in the story because that had more connotations for me. Over time, I started thinking, *Who is this Anne Rey?* And that's how the story developed. It was a process of a couple of years.

"As I mulled over the idea, things began to hook up, other seed ideas that I would read in my journal or copy down. I had an idea from a year later about a guy living on a sailboat, giving up most everything and going off to live on a sailboat. I also copied down some interesting notes from a lecture I heard on art restoration. So, one day, in reviewing my journals and thinking about story ideas, all of a sudden I was reading the-guy-on-the-sailboat story, and I realized it's not a story about a guy living on a sailboat. It's Anne Rey who lives on the sailboat. That's who she is. And then I was reading more and I realized she's an art restorer. That's it! So those three things started coming together, and then the fourth key thing was a year later—I had an experience. I was making films at the time and I was doing a film on radiology. I was interviewing patients for this film, and there was a woman who told me about the experience that she'd had of feeling that there was—and I'm quoting her—'a strange little hat' on her head, the pressure of a little hat on her head. And she'd had a lot of radiological studies done because sometimes the sense of phantom pressure can be the sign of a tumor. So she had a series of CAT scans but they never found anything. She still felt the pressure. That story kind of made an impression on me, and eventually she became the mother, complete with little phantom hats, a woman who was slowly going insane, Anne Rey's mother. So there are about four different things there, things that happened to me, things that I heard people say, things that I saw, that happened over the course of two years, that then came together, mixing and matching, to feed into and become the story 'Anne Rey'."

Here then is the opening of Kaplan's story:

> When Anne Rey was a little girl and her mother read her fairy tales from a large purple book, her favorites had been those in which the hero embarked on a journey by boat; in later years, after consulting the I Ching, Anne always felt a special thrill when she received a hexagram advising "crossing a great sea." So perhaps it was not surprising that shortly after her mother began complaining about the "funny little hat" on the side of her head, Anne Rey—twenty-eight years old, single, art restorer, specializing in prints and drawings—decided to give up her small apartment and move onto a sailboat.

That process of mixing and matching is exactly what fiction writers do, whether the story is based on real life or not. This kind of transformation is central to the fiction process. And when you write about someone real, this mixing and matching isn't merely good for self-protection; it deepens your understanding of the character by involving your imaginative process. It makes the character your own "Anne Rey," not the Anne Ray you spotted on a license plate.

One might argue that simply mashing together aspects of different people's personalities is not an act of the imagination at all, but that's a foolish notion. The test of one's imagination is not simply in one's ability to invent details and characters out of thin air, but also in how one orders and overlays real events and people, how one transforms real life into something completely new.

For example, the episode of the ghost I mentioned earlier is something that a student and her sister told me once about their father. When he was a boy, he had an uncle who would sometimes stay with the family. The uncle kept a bottle of whiskey hidden in the boy's dresser, and late at night he'd sneak in and take a swig, and the boy would watch him. Then one night, the uncle came into the room and just looked down at the boy in his bed, but didn't take any whiskey or say anything. The next day the boy learned that his uncle had died that night in a car accident. But the story goes on. Every night for a month, the uncle visited the boy, just staring down at him. The family still owns that house, and the father of my student refuses to spend the night there.

The other details I mentioned, about the elderly man whose sister cooks for him every night—that's the relationship between my Uncle Morty and my Grandmother Ida, both of whom are no longer alive. Every night he'd come over and she'd cook dinner for him, and then he'd leave with hardly a word. Of course, there's nothing terribly revealing or troubling or even all that interesting in the situation, and if I'd wanted to write about Morty and Ida and their nightly ritual when they were alive, I would have done so without any compunction whatsoever. It's only when I overlaid something else on top of these people—the ghost sighting—that the story started becoming somewhat intriguing.

Remember that all of these people are or were real, but probably none of them would have recognized themselves in the context in which I placed them. I took my real relatives and added details from the life of a complete stranger, a man I've never even met.

Of course, maybe I'm fooling you again. Maybe I have no Uncle Morty or Grandmother Ida. Maybe I never had a student whose father saw a ghost. The truth of it shouldn't matter to you. Is it interesting? Is it believable? Those are the only issues that count.

WRITING WITHOUT COMPOSITES

Sometimes a writer will bravely, or foolishly, decide to write about a family member or friend without transforming that person much, if at all. It's difficult enough to write in the first place. It's murder when you also have to worry about how Aunt Elena will take it when she inevitably sees the story you've written, based on her life. I'm assuming a negative reaction here, but I've found that people are rarely as upset about being included in your stories as you think they'll be. Often, your Aunt Elena won't recognize herself, or, if she does, she'll ignore those aspects of herself that might have been portrayed negatively.

When Thomas Wolfe first wrote *Look Homeward, Angel*, his hometown of Asheville ostracized him because he wrote about them and told their secrets. He couldn't even show his face in Asheville. A few years after the book was published and he was a world-famous author, the only people who were mad at him were those he didn't include in the book.

Another Asheville native, Gail Godwin, wrote an early novel, *The Old Woman*, in which her younger sister and her mother were cast as characters, though somewhat transformed. In her essay "Becoming a Writer," Godwin recalls that her sister complained, "She'd better never put me in a novel again. I don't like being frozen in print for the rest of my life, forever wearing those silly panties and short skirts; and I'm *not* big like that, she's made me into some sort of Amazon freak." Godwin's mother was more understanding, saying obviously the character based on her was too stupid and passive to be an accurate reflection. The young Godwin responded that the character *was* supposed to be her mother. "Well, there was something left out, then," her mother said.

Novelist Bret Lott hardly transformed his family at all in his novel *Jewel* (Pocket Books), a story based on his grandmother's life. The story is about a woman who finally has to break the spirit and the will of her husband, and to sacrifice much of the childhood of her five other children for the sixth one, a down's syndrome child. When the book was published, he went to his grandmother's house. She was happy to see him, of course, then took him out on the patio behind the house and sat him down at the picnic table and said, "Well, it's a beautiful book, but I just want to tell you I wasn't as hard on your grandfather as you made me out to be." Lott was taken aback. "I said, 'Grandma, it's a novel,' which is always the novelist's excuse, so I was able to weasel my way out of this. Because it was so known in our family that I was writing this book about her and the family, I don't think that she saw a difference between the book and the true family story, which is a dangerous thing — especially since in the novel I used everyone's name. Those are the true names of everyone. I got permission from everyone to do that, but I just couldn't do any better than the real names: Jewel, Leston, Wilman, Burton, Billie Jean, Ann, Brenda Kay. So in her mind, the delineation between fiction and the truth was very blurry. But the other side of the story is that every sibling, every one of her children, all those people involved have said to me at one time or another, 'You got that exactly right.' She, in fact, did break the spirit of her husband, my grandfather. This was a truth she did not necessarily want to face."

With Lott's first novel, *The Man Who Owned Vermont* (Viking), he had to face the disapproval of his father: "*The Man Who Owned Vermont* is about an R.C. Cola salesman. My dad's life was R.C. Cola. He was an R.C. Cola man from 1951 to 1982. When you read that novel, it's a pretty disparaging account of what it's like to be a soda pop salesman. The character doesn't believe in doing what he does, so the whole thing's a sham. There's a line in there about how his whole life has been about selling something that no one in their right mind would want. Chemicals and carbonated water and caramel coloring. Who really needs this? My dad has said on many occasions, 'I know you think that selling soda pop was a waste.' I told him it's not true. All I could say was, 'Dad, it's a novel.' "

Getting Permission

Sometimes, you've got to give yourself permission to write about your Aunt Elenas, your Jewels, your moms and dads. If you want to write a story about a relative or close friend, but feel some hesitation, ask yourself why. Are you sure that your friend or relative will recognize herself? If so, can you change anything about her to make her less recognizable. If not, maybe you should just go to the person you want to write about and ask for her permission. If she says no, you'll have to respect her wishes or perhaps lose her favor. But part of her response will depend on how you phrase the question. If you act sheepish about it and make it seem like a horrible thing, you can expect a defensive, negative reaction. If you explain a little bit about the story, that it's fiction, and that her life is fascinating to you and worthy of exploration, her reaction will probably be positive. But there's no guarantee. Nor is there any hard-and-fast rule about getting people's permission, but we'll get into ethical and legal questions later.

Remember that there's a certain amount of courage involved in writing, and if you always stay with material that's safe and won't get you into any trouble (even if the trouble is only with your own conflicting emotions about uncovering material that's close to home), your writing might ultimately seem limited and dull. Good writing takes risks and sometimes unsettles the writer as well as the reader. Fiction does not necessarily reflect the world as it should be, but as it is, and that means chronicling conflict. In real life, most of us avoid conflict. But conflict is a crucial element of all fiction, as it is an element of life. Imperfect beings that we are, we thrive on conflict, whether it's the base, reptilian conflict of a car blowing up at the end of a chase scene in a movie, or the more subtle, psychological conflict of a contemporary short story.

Fiction often deals with people making moral choices, and sometimes making the wrong ones. If you write about the world as it is, and not as you'd like it to be, you will definitely offend someone, and not necessarily your Aunt Elena. As Flannery O'Connor put it, storytelling is "an attempt to make someone who doesn't want to listen, listen, and who doesn't want to see, see. We can't change what we see to suit the reader, but we must convey it as whole as possible into his unspacious quarters for his divided and suspicious consideration."

It's important, however, to avoid being too solipsistic in one's writing, thinking that people exist simply as fodder for your brilliant novels and stories. Donald Barthelme explores this notion in his story "The Author," which deals with a mother blithely uncovering the family skeletons of her grown children in her novels. She portrays one of her sons, a doctor, hanging out with a bunch of survivalists in Miami. She also reveals her daughter Virginia's car accident in which Virginia's blood-alcohol ratio was .18 percent. Another son threatens to sue her for writing of his habit of purchasing "U.S. Army morphine syrettes from disaffected Medical Corps master sergeants." The narrator, a former museum-curator-at-large, has been let go because of his mother's uncovering of his theft of several "inconsequential" Native American medicine bundles from the museum. When he confronts his mother, asks her why and how she can do what she does, she answers him coolly, "Because you're mine."

ACTING THE PART

No matter whom you base your characters on, you must think of yourself as much as an actor as a writer. You need to get into the role and learn your part. That's why details are so important, the small details that make up someone's life. One of the best ways to understand characters and motivation is to take an acting class. Of course, most good writers come to their understanding of things such as motivation intuitively; just as many have never read Freud but intuitively understand the concepts of displacement and projection.

A writer, just like an actor, needs to believe the character she is writing about. If you aren't convinced your character is real (whether based on your Uncle Lou or your friend's Uncle Shorty or made up whole cloth), your reader certainly won't believe either.

I'm not saying that the Uncle Shorty in your story should be a photocopy of the real Uncle Shorty. But you should be able to answer any question, no matter how seemingly insignificant, about your character. If asked, "What do the curtains in Shorty's bedroom look like?" you should be able to answer, "There aren't any curtains in his bedroom," or whatever you think best fits his character. It's not necessary that all of these details make it into your story. It's important that you know your character well enough to supply these details. Above all, you want your characters, no matter whom they're based on, to seem as though they lived and breathed before the opening paragraph of your story. You want them to have a sense of history.

Finding the Right Details

Whether a character in your story or novel is wholly imagined, partly imagined, or a true-to-life representation of someone doesn't matter at all. What matters is the character's believability to the reader. Being believable is not the same as being realistic. Plenty of writers pull off having outlandish characters and plots and settings in their stories, because they make their characters and the worlds they live in believable through *salient details* — that is, physical, sensory details that make the character stand out in the reader's mind. We experience life through our senses, so it stands to reason that if we try to recreate life through the writing of fiction, using sensory details will help create an illusion of real-life experience.

When you write about a character, you must choose the details that will fix him in the reader's mind. Simply writing a sentence like "Uncle Lou was a big man," does not make him a memorable character. How big was he? "The only pants Uncle Lou ever felt comfortable in were second-hand maternity slacks." Now there's a sentence that shows a couple of things about Uncle Lou. It shows perhaps a kind of absurd frugality on his part, as well as giving one a pretty fair idea of how big he is.

When you write about a real person, especially someone you know quite well, a flood of details usually will hit you, many more than you can possibly use in your story. Write as many of those details down in your journal as possible, but select the few that will firmly anchor the character in our minds. If the remarkable thing about Uncle Lou was his shoe size (maybe he wore a size fifteen), make that the detail that types him. Maybe several things made your uncle remarkable — not only his foot size, but he had an enormous beard, never washed his hair and wore a greasy Cleveland Indians baseball cap. Perhaps you can get away with using all those details, but you might have to toss one or two of them to make him less of a caricature. Which ones would you choose to drop? You'd choose different ones from the ones I'd choose. But the more specific a detail, the more memorable it will be to the reader, and that's a good rule of thumb to use when deciding which details to include in your fiction and which to get rid of.

Likewise, you don't have to give us all these details at once. In fact, if you do, they'll blur, and we'll have as indistinct an impression of your character as if you'd given us no details at all. As a writer of fiction, you must learn to slowly dispense information about your characters, not all in a rush, never to be mentioned again. If, for instance, you decide to keep the greasy baseball cap, it should have some role in the story. Same with the foot size. Not only should it give us some sense of who your character is, but, if possible, make it part of your story's plot. Otherwise, the baseball cap becomes a red herring, a false clue, a detail that serves no purpose other than the author's whim.

TYPE VERSUS STEREOTYPE

Type is different from stereotype. Certain things are typical of people without necessarily being stereotypical. A plumber, for instance, will usually have typical tools of the trade: a plumber's snake, a truck or van, a jumpsuit of some kind for crawling around basements, a flashlight. So what's a stereotype of a plumber? Probably the first two or three images that come to mind are negative, since stereotypes are usually unfair and demeaning—overcharging or falling-down pants. That's not to say that such stereotypes are completely false and nonexistent in real life, just that they're stale, overused and unfair. That's what a stereotype is, an unoriginal image of a person or group of people, most often used in a derogatory fashion.

Just because you've met someone who fits a stereotype doesn't mean that he'll be less of a stereotype when you place him in a story. In a piece of fiction, *avoid stereotypes*. The reason should seem obvious. Besides the fact that denigrating other people is not the nicest thing in the world, why bother to reinforce old stereotypes, to write about things that have been said a thousand times before? Fictional characters must seem complex for us to believe they're flesh and blood. Real live flesh-and-blood characters don't have to seem complex at all. If you have a friend with a pickup with fat tires, a gun rack, a bumper sticker that reads, "American by birth, Southern by the grace of God," and a blue-tick hound dog named Otis who rides in back, you might say, "Wow, what a stereotype, but he's still my bud." But if you put your bud in a story, I might say, "Sorry, too much of a stereotype. Make him more realistic." And you say, "How? If I make him more realistic, I'll be fictionalizing him." And I'll say, "Exactly!"

HISTORICAL FIGURES AND CELEBRITIES

Sometimes writers of fiction use historical figures or celebrities in their stories. Barry Hannah, while by no means a writer of historical fiction, has made forays into the area. In his acclaimed short story collection, *Airships* (Random House), three stories deal with Jeb Stuart, the Confederate general. "Jeb Stuart attracted me because he was so unlike me," Hannah says. "He was a twenty-nine-year-old general. He was a Presbyterian who didn't smoke or drink. He was very dashing, the last of the cavalry heroes. He just about embodies everything good about the South that I know of, and about the cavalier era.

"When I wrote about Jeb after I'd read a good deal about him, I was interested in those around him, the effect that a hero has on those close to him. So I used what I knew about him but I also made up my own cast of folks to put around him. There's one gay guy. I don't think a gay Confederate had ever been written about."

Like any kind of fiction, you must have the confidence to use your imagination, to transform the historical figure or current celebrity—to make the character your own. You're mucking around in history and that can be a daunting challenge to a timid writer. But if you attempt such a story, remember that it's fiction you're writing, not history. And, depending on what your goals are in the story, you don't necessarily have to stick to the facts of your subject's life. If your aims are absurdist, you can write a story about how Judy Garland, at the decline of her career, took up sumo wrestling. Obviously, that's nowhere near the truth of her life. But a number of writers have written stories like that to great effect. These stories tend to be more cultural metaphors than actual explorations of someone's life. That's not to say that the two are mutually exclusive. Barry Hannah's stories about Jeb Stuart have as much to do metaphorically with the cultures of the old and new South as they do with the actual life of Jeb Stuart.

"The reason you can use your imagination," says Hannah, "is that most history is not in the books. Their day-to-day life is not in the books. You only get a gloss. It's not that my guess is as good as any, because I try to be educated about the era. But it is up for grabs about what a guy is like in a given hour. People are not always postured and heroic. And they say dreadful things, even the best people. But they sure don't make speeches. And they have to get up and put their pants on. That part of history is never in the books. And I like to give a sense of it."

The main thing to remember when writing this kind of fiction is to do your research. Know something about the era. Know something about the person. Go to the library and look at microfilm of newspaper articles about the person you're writing about. Read biographies about the person, not just one, but two or three. Biographers don't necessarily agree with one another, so you can usually get a couple of different perspectives by reading more than one, and then you can decide which is the most accurate — or you can invent your own perspective. To some degree, you must create your own perspective, or else the story will simply be warmed-over biography.

The way you introduce your famous character in such a story or novel is perhaps of more importance than in any other kind of fiction. If you're not careful, you can easily alienate the reader. If you simply rely on stereotypes of your famous character, or introduce him in a sensational manner, you can be sure that your reader will not be convinced. Consider this opening:

> Napoleon sat at his dresser, hand in his jacket, admiring himself in the mirror.

This is a silly opening, starting out in the most obvious fashion. On the other hand, better not to keep your reader unaware of your famous subject's identity too long. Your reader's reaction might be a groan when she discovers after thirty pages who your subject is.

Einstein's Dreams, a novel by Alan Lightman (Pantheon), recreates in an almost impressionistic form Einstein's discovery of the nature of time. Here is the way it opens:

> In some distant arcade, a clock tower calls out six times and then stops. The young man slumps at his desk. He has come to the office at dawn, after another upheaval. His hair is uncombed and his trousers are too big. In his hand, he holds twenty crumpled pages, his new theory of time, which he will mail today to the German journal of physics.

Several things make this opening convincing. Obviously, we know the subject by the title of the book, and in that first paragraph he's not mentioned by name. He doesn't need to be mentioned by name, because Einstein is a universally famous figure, and the reader brings a certain amount of knowledge to the story already. The theory of time is a dead giveaway, as is the slight physical description of the young man's appearance, especially the uncombed hair. The reader instantly recalls the famous photo of an older Einstein with his hair going in all directions at once. The more famous your subject, the less you have to dwell on the obvious facts about that person.

Also notice that the author casts his story in present tense. This strategy gives us a sense of immediacy. It's as though we're watching a movie unfold in slow motion with both sound and sight involved: the distant tolling of the clock, the visual image of the man slumped over his desk. Casting the paragraph in third person, objective, also adds to the sense of a cool authority giving us this information, the facts, as they were, without any interpretation — or so it would seem. It would be hard to come up with a better strategy for introducing such a famous man to us. And it's all done through salient details and a subtle handling of the information we must know about this character.

Exercises

1. Choose a profession. Make a list of stereotypes of that profession. Then make a list of things that are typical to that profession. Now write a scene including some, though not all, of your typical list and none of your stereotypical list. To make the character seem more real, model him on someone you've actually known or observed in that profession or a similar one.

2. Recall someone you know well—a friend, a relative—preferably someone who's a bit eccentric, someone with strong personality traits. Identify two or three of those personality traits and list them at the top of the page. Now create a scene that shows these personality traits in your friend or relative—but never mention these personality traits. Try to convey them with dialogue, action and salient detail. So, if your Uncle Lou is childlike, forgetful and generous, show him as such in the scene. But try to avoid easy stereotypes of generosity, forgetfulness, etc.

3. Write a scene using this same character, but transform her into a new character. Change one or two of her personality traits. Combine her with another friend or relative. Change her name, age, gender. Use your imagination so that what you end up with is *based* on your friend or relative but is not that person at all anymore.

4. Write a scene from the point of view of someone famous whose life you know fairly well. Don't dwell so much in the scene on what made him famous, but on what made him ordinary, on the particulars of his life.

5. Interview a relative. Ask her to recall a particular year. Just pick one arbitrarily, say, 1939. Ask your relative to recall that year in as much detail as possible: what was going on in the world, what was going on in the country, in the state, in the city, on the block, in the family, with herself. As you narrow your questions, a stronger

and stronger portrait will begin to emerge. After you've finished the interview, write a scene with your relative in it, set in the year you focused on in the interview. Pick and choose the salient details to make both your relative and the world of 1939 come alive. Is this the beginning of a story?

CHAPTER FIVE

Real Stories

E ven if you're ostensibly writing something autobiographical, you're still an actor taking on a role, and the hardest role to play is yourself. John Barth has a story that skewers the whole notion of autobiographical fiction, called "Life-Story." It's an infuriating little story about a man writing a story called "Life-Story," all about a man who's writing a story called "Life-Story," and so on ad infinitum. The disappearing mirrors trick. It's a story about a man who can't even get enough distance from his first line to write a story.

What we're saying here is that if you base something on real life, you must resign yourself to the fact that you won't be able to tell the whole truth and nothing but the truth. Writing from real life is a constant dialogue between one's memory and one's imagination. You must give your imagination room to roam if you want to write fiction from real life successfully. You must be flexible with your life, which is easier said than done. In her essay, "Becoming a Writer," Gail Godwin writes: "Fact and fiction: fiction and fact. At what point does regurgitated autobiography graduate into memory shaped by art? How do you know when to stop telling it as it is, or was, and make it into what it ought to be — or what would make a better story" In this chapter, we'll explore different types of fiction derived from fact, and strategies for turning real-life experiences into fiction.

Ever since Hemingway, some writers have latched onto the silly notion that you must experience life before you can write about it. That's not true, at least not in the narrow sense of experience. Flannery O'Connor said we have enough to write about for the rest of our lives if we survive childhood. It's not important whether you've actually fished for wahoo off the coast of North Carolina or saw a blue-footed Booby in St. Augustine. What you need is enough depth and range in your character and imagination to make us believe in the experience of the story. That's the only experience that counts: the reader's experience of the story, whether he believes you or not, whether you've created a virtual reality much more advanced than any computer will ever be capable of.

Many beginning fiction writers seem to want to be journalists. Most journalists will swear that they're after the truth when the fact is that many journalists seem to be pretty good at fictionalizing, whether they mean to or not. Ask anyone who has ever been interviewed. Or the next time there's a disaster, flip the channels and see how wildly the accounts can differ. Any basic philosophy class will teach you that truth is in the perceptions of the viewer. So why do you care anyway what really happened in your life? Does the fact that it happened make it more important? Does it make it a better story? Fiction writers are after a different kind of truth from journalists, though no less important, and perhaps ultimately more honest. Fiction writers are after what Faulkner called "the eternal verities," certainly a highfalutin term, but fine for him. After all, he was Faulkner. You, on the other hand, probably shouldn't go around saying that you want to write eternal verities, or people might slap you.

Ironically enough, in our quest for verities, we must often lie. Ask the successful liar what her main ingredient is, and she will probably tell you that you must believe the lie you're telling. You must convince yourself it's true, be earnest about it, or else the listener certainly won't believe you. Lying, like life, is in the details. What really happened is irrelevant. You must look at your life as almost a great patchwork. In an article in *The New York Times Book Review* about author Henry Roth, Leonard Michaels states that Roth "begins with small factual events, then imagines their emotional consequences and finally gives them an imaginative expression that may be far from the original events." In a letter to *The New York Times Book Review*, author Susan Fromberg Schaeffer puts it quite eloquently when she writes that "fiction is a record of that conflagration that occurs when reality collides with imagination." *There's* a quote worth taping above your writing desk.

Sherwood Anderson gives us a glimpse of this conflagration in "Death in the Woods," the story of an old, unloved woman, who's been abused by one man after another until she collapses and freezes to death one day on her long walk from town to her farm. Her abuse starts early in her life. She is orphaned and spends her youth in servitude to a cruel farmer. Later, her husband and son treat her miserably. Her death in the woods is attended only by a pack of wild dogs who skitter and yap around her as she slips into death. They then tear the clothes from her body.

Toward the end of his story, the narrator suddenly intrudes and tells how, as a young boy, he and his brother accompanied a group of men to recover the body of an old woman frozen in the snow. And then, remarkably, he tells us how this later worked itself into his story:

> I remember only the picture there in the forest, the men standing about, the naked girlish-looking figure, face down in the snow, the tracks made by the running dogs and the clear cold winter sky above . . .
>
> The scene in the forest had become for me, without my knowing it, the foundation for the real story I am now trying to tell. The fragments, you see, had to be picked up slowly, long afterward.
>
> Things happened. When I was a young man I worked on the farm of a German. The hired girl was afraid of her employer. The farmer's wife hated her.
>
> I saw things at that place. Once later, I had a half-uncanny, mystical adventure with dogs in an Illinois forest on a clear, moonlit winter night. . . . The whole thing, the story of the old woman's death, was to me as I grew older like music heard from far off. The notes had to be picked up slowly one at a time. Something had to be understood.

All you really need to know about writing stories based on your life is encapsulated in the above passage. The notes have to picked up slowly one at a time. Something has to be understood.

GENERATING IDEAS

After a reading, I'm sometimes asked, "Where do your ideas come from?" Ideas come from any number of sources, from dreams to snatches of overheard conversation to family stories. Another variation on this question is, "How do you keep generating ideas?" The answer to that one is easy: "By staying alive." The more you write, the more you naturally generate ideas. A teacher once told me that all you had to do to get story material is to look around, to keep your eyes open. That might sound easy, but it's not. Usually, we're stuck in our everyday routines and notice very little about the world around us, or, if we notice it, it's in a familiar, unsurprised way. The writer, on the other hand, must try to notice what's new in the familiar, to look upon the world as if encountering it for the first time. That's why children are so naturally imaginative. They don't know the world's boundaries. They don't have expectations. If you have expectations, if you know that the tree in front of your house is only the same old tree you see every day, you probably won't have any new ideas. On the other hand, ask yourself some questions about the tree. What exactly is the view that the tree obscures? Does it block the view of your neighbor's kitchen window? Who are your neighbors? Who planted the tree?

For most writers, ideas are not the problem. It's the follow-through. Some people say that nothing interesting has ever happened to them, so they have nothing to write about. But I don't buy that. Even if you've stayed in one place your entire life, on the same street, in the same house — that doesn't necessarily mean your life is trivial and boring. Perhaps you take it for granted. You've stopped paying attention. And if you want to write, you must pay attention.

If it's been a while since you've written a story, or if you've never written a story before, your imagination might be a little rusty, or your self-confidence might be low. In that case, go back to your journal. Brainstorm. List the names of five people you haven't seen in five years or more. Why haven't you seen them? List five lies you've told. What were their consequences? List five lies you wished you'd told. What do all of these exercises have in common? They all have a kernel of conflict within them, at least potentially, and conflict is a central ingredient of any story. You don't have to use these exercises. Anything that sparks your memory, that sparks your interest, will do.

FLEXIBILITY

If you want to write a story about a family vacation you took in 1976, think of all the other vacations you took as a family, even ones you took alone. Glue them in your mind. Use only what's helpful from one memory and then discard the rest. And now that we're on the subject, is it important that the story take place in 1976? Is there anything to justify the time other than that really was the year you and the kids or your parents or whomever decided to take that trip to Yellowstone? If that's the only reason, back up. You're not thinking like a fiction writer.

But the year is crucial to the story, you say. It couldn't take place in any other year. The story is called "Bicentennial," and it involves two brothers in a sailboat who are on their way to try to view the tall ships as they come into New York's harbor on the Fourth of July. Furthermore, the story is about the younger brother's preoccupation with his own independence and the older one's more wistful feelings about the bonds to his family. That sounds a tad heavy-handed to me, but it's your story. If you want to set it in 1976 and believe you can justify it, go to it.

Flexibility is perhaps the most important ingredient for a successful story based on real life. It's not so much a strategy as it is a state of mind. If you are unwilling or unable to change events in a story because "they really happened," you don't want to write fiction. If you are unwilling to revise your story, the prognosis is likewise bleak. Always remember that you're writing fiction, whether based on fact or not, and look for the story that didn't happen within the story that did.

GETTING DISTANCE

Not *everything* that happens to you can or needs to be fictionalized. It's unhealthy and a little creepy for one to think of everything that happens as possible fodder for one's fiction. That kind of attitude can lead to some pretty serious self-absorption. Unfortunately, we've all met writers or artists who seem to view themselves as little gods who breathe more rarefied air than the rest of us mortals. After a traumatic event, the last thing one should be thinking about is one's fiction.

Some people think of writing as therapeutic. Maybe on some level it is, but if you need therapy, see a therapist. Writing, if anything, will make you more neurotic.

If you write about a traumatic event, you generally need distance. If your parents died in a plane crash yesterday, do you really think you're ready to begin writing a short story about the event today? Is a year too soon? Three years? Why are you writing the story in the first place? To honor your parents? To help you through your grief? Or because it would make a good story? The third reason is the only correct answer. Perhaps that might sound cold to you but remember, we're talking about fiction. A story is not powerful simply because it happened to or is important to the writer. But perhaps we need to make a distinction here between private writing and public writing. Privately, you can write whatever you want, in whatever form and for whatever reason. But once you bring that story into the world, once you seek an audience for it, the audience is under no obligation to be kind or sympathetic, or to like what you have written. Imagine how you would feel if you showed your story to an acquaintance, and she said, "Boy, what wicked characters. I'm so relieved the parents died in that plane crash. They deserved it!"

You need distance as well to judge whether your parents' death in a fiery plane crash would make a good story. Chances are it won't. It's tragic and horrible, but those elements alone don't make a good story. One problem is that people who are trying to deal with traumatic events feel a kind of ownership of the material, which can make a writer inflexible. Nothing can be written in stone. Everything must be subject to revision, and a sure sign that you're too close to your subject is the feeling that you want to be true to the subject, that you don't want to change a word. "I think thematically it would work better if the parents died in a speedboat accident," your acquaintance says. If you refuse to consider the suggestion only on the grounds that it didn't happen that way, go back to the chapter on memoirs.

One achieves distance through the passage of time, but there are some strategies to help you along. If you write about a place you've lived in, leaving it sometimes gives you the best perspective. Change the gender of the main character. Or the age. Change the point of view. Change anything that will make the character *not you*. It's important that you don't think of your main character as yourself. The character can be based on you, but you must make a distinction. Otherwise, you might be unwilling to allow things to happen to the character that you wouldn't want happening to yourself, or allow your character to behave in a way you wouldn't normally behave. And the point of writing a story is not to impress everyone with what a good or heroic person you are.

INDIRECTION

Often, stories deal best with the aftermath of trauma rather than the unfolding of it. Instead of ending your story with a horrific car accident, try beginning your story with it, as Robley Wilson Jr. skillfully does in his short story "Favorites," which opens with the death of a man's wife in a car accident.

> On a Saturday afternoon in September his wife was killed in a car accident. As the state police explained it to him, she had finished her grocery shopping and was pulling out onto the highway in front of the shopping center when a young man in a pickup truck slammed into her car. The impact was just behind the driver's door, she died instantly, never knew what hit her—things people say in such circumstances, things the police told him. The young man wasn't hurt; he was drunk and stoned, and charges against him were pending. Very sorry. The car was written off as a total loss.

After he gets the trauma out of the way, Wilson is able to focus on his main character, the husband. Instead of focusing on the large event, Wilson chooses something much smaller and seemingly inconsequential. It seems that the woman's last words to her husband were, "I made your favorite dessert." The story deals with the man's consumption of his wife's final treat for him. That's called *indirection*, approaching the trauma sideways rather than head-on. The way he delicately eats this dessert over a period of several days is a powerful and ingenious way of showing the man's grief and love for his wife.

This method works especially well with short stories. By definition, short stories are short and tend to be somewhat fragile in their construction. The main problem is that your writing will seem melodramatic if you try to pack an emotional wallop in an unsophisticated way. If you focus solely on the traumatic event as it's unfolding, say, a car accident you were in as a child, this event might likely overwhelm your characters, and the story will become merely seamy rather than emotionally powerful.

Life *can* be melodramatic, and there's nothing wrong with extreme shows of emotion if, say, you watch your parents' plane burst into flame high above the field where they were practicing looptyloops in front of your eyes. But fiction isn't real life. It's artifice, and what works in real life doesn't always work in fiction.

Some people might be horrified by what they consider the "matter-of-fact" tone of a story such as "Favorites." Look at that first paragraph again. There *is* a certain distance and irony to the words, especially phrases like, "Very sorry," but that doesn't mean that the story is bloodless and unemotional. When you reach the final paragraph of this story, it's hard to read aloud without your voice cracking a bit.

> One night only a single piece of his wife's dessert remained. He cut it in half. The following night he cut the half in half. Then he must have realized what he was doing, for on the third night he ate all that was left of the dessert — luscious, irreplaceable treat — and set the empty pan to soak in the kitchen sink.

Another distinction I'd like to draw here is one between cheap sentimentality and true sentiment. Sentimentality pulls at your heart strings in an obnoxious clichéd manner: images of orphans crying in the rain or puppy dogs wandering the streets in search of a loving home. True, these occurrences are heart-breaking in real life, but not terribly original in fiction. Leave them to the six o'clock news. Conversely, the emotional punch of a truly good story will sneak up on you. It'll be unpredictable and twice as powerful, because you didn't know it was there waiting for you.

The paradox is that sometimes the more you leave out, the more you hold back, and the more tension is created in the reader's mind while she waits for that release of emotion or catharsis. If you have a constant catharsis on the page, characters screaming as blood gushes out of their wounds at the scene of a horrible accident, the reader will soon become bored and numbed by the steady shrill tone of your prose, just as we are numbed by the six o'clock news. A constant release of emotional energy works against the natural form of the short story—the rising action or building of tension leading to the climax.

This doesn't mean you should avoid trauma. Just avoid having characters react to the trauma in a predictable way. You want your reader to think, "Why aren't you reacting like a normal human being? Where are your tears!'?" just as the director of a horror film wants the audience to think, "No, don't go up those stairs, stupid!"

When I say a writer needs distance, that doesn't at all mean the writing should be unemotional and bloodless. It's just that if you're too close to the event, you might have a tendency to gush, when holding back might be what's necessary to make the story emotionally powerful.

Novels are different. A novel can more easily handle what in a short story might seem melodramatic if faced head-on. A novelist has more space in which to explore his characters and their reactions to the events, harrowing as they may be. If the trauma is explored over several hundred pages, it runs less of a risk of seeming melodramatic. The more you examine the trauma, the more you're able to convince and draw the reader into the full depths of such an emotional experience. A good example of this is Dorothy Allison's novel of child abuse and neglect in the dirt-poor rural South, *Bastard out of Carolina* (Dutton).

THE HEAD-ON APPROACH

Most writers will, at some point, put a sentence down on paper that makes them uncomfortable, that seems to reveal too much. Faulkner, in accepting his Nobel Prize, spoke of "the human heart in conflict with itself, which alone can make good writing because only that is worth writing about, worth the agony and the sweat."

The worst kind of writing, and much of it is published, even cele-brated, is fiction that takes no risks, that makes the reader comfort-able about the world he lives in—fiction that reinforces our easy assumptions of the world. Good fiction often deals with moral am-bivalence, not easy answers; with unfortunate or ambiguous choices resulting not in clear-cut victories or happy Hollywood endings, but haunting, sometimes troubling resolutions.

Some writers tackle the most painful subjects head-on and throw indirection out the window. This is more a personality issue than one of craft. One writer who writes on the edge, who often goes for the jugular rather than the comforts of indirection, is Sharon Solwitz. Solwitz is able to write about life's most dramatic moments without teetering into melodrama. And she's able to write about subjects that are painfully close to her. She says of her work, "When I first started, I used to take something that was interesting from the past that I had distance on. So I wrote a lot of stories about when I was a teenager or kid. That's a kind of a natural distance you have. But now, often lately, when I'm feeling kind of tense about something, when I feel an issue is unresolved, I take the issue that's right in front of me. And I write it."

Even in those early stories, she still went for the material that was most likely to deal with her own secrets and fears. For those wishing to write this way, she suggests starting with a line that gives you goose bumps. She adds, however, that "the most unendurable pieces of writing are by writers who try to work out their problems on paper without the benefit of craft. A character whines for ten pages about her need for love, and we want to close the book just as we'd want to switch seats on the bus to avoid such a relentlessly confessional new acquaintance.

"But there's something to be said for the thrill of dealing with red-hot conflict, transforming it. Much of it will be rant and rave, but sometimes the metamorphosis will happen right then and there, and you'll know it."

An example of this unusual ability is her story, "If You Step on a Crack . . ." based on a real-life experience. When Solwitz found a lump in her breast, and it was biopsied, she was, of course, terri-fied. So she wrote a story that mirrored her situation. Both Solwitz and her protagonist are married, mother of twin boys, Seth and Jesse in Solwitz's case, Seth and Simon in the story. Both live a couple of hundred feet from Wrigley Field in Chicago. Both have problems with baseball fans relieving themselves in the alley below their house.

The story works beautifully and was published in the magazine *Tikkun*. Solwitz writes in a cool, often witty style that creates distance without sacrificing any of the emotion of the moment. Instead of starting with the trauma of "Is the tumor malignant or not?" Solwitz deflects the trauma a bit by beginning with the lighter problem of drunken fans relieving themselves in the alley.

> Her first and only husband sat on the couch in front of the pregame interview. From four doors south across Waveland Avenue the lights of Wrigley Field cast their salmon glow on his long-sleeved shirt. Three stories down, the steps of Cub and Cardinal fans crunched along the alley, overlaid by spates of mild, ritualized jeering. Blue and red caps bobbed toward the bleacher entrance. "Come let's cheer them on to ignominy," said Andy, to whom she had been married longer than any of her friends to their husbands. He held out his hand.
>
> She had been watching a golden-haired boy of twenty or so take a whiz in the alley. "What fun," she said, to either, to both.

After a page or so, she introduces the greater twin dilemmas of her possible breast cancer and her husband's seeming indifference. This is a wise strategy, whether dealing with recent or long-past trauma. You don't have to let the reader know everything about the situation and the crisis in the story right away. There's a certain amount of timing involved in divulging important information about a character. You don't want to wait too long to tell the reader, like the last line of the story. "Oh, by the way. I'm a dromedary. You've been reading the words of a camel all along. Ha ha!" Then your story resorts to cheap gimmicks. Moreover, you don't have to tell everything about the conflict of the story in the first paragraph. Slowly divulging such information, especially if it's somewhat traumatic, can, if your timing is right, lend even more tension to the story.

In the story, the protagonist doesn't learn the results of her test.

Another good strategy on Solwitz's part. Whether she has breast cancer is not the issue of the story. It might be why some readers are reading, but that's not the same thing. The central conflict is between the protagonist and her husband. As in any story, what's most important are the characters and what we learn about them, and by inference, human nature as a result of this traumatic situation. If the power of your story relies only on a dramatic question (does she have cancer?) rather than on the characters, your story probably will be melodramatic rather than having true emotional intensity, as Solwitz achieves in her story.

"It could have been a terrible cliché," says Solwitz. "A woman is afraid of breast cancer. She has a biopsy. Outcome: Either she has it or she doesn't. She's disfigured or she isn't. She lives or dies. I imagine I could have gotten the reader involved because of the unfortunate universality of the experience. But I knew even as I was conceiving it that the yes or no answer, she lives or dies — neither would ultimately satisfy. We're all helpless in the face of good news or bad news and the writer can't fix that.

"Transformation involved moving away from the cliché of the tension of the possibly terrible outcome. The not-knowing became only a psychological setting turned into the background. Foregrounded was first her relationship with her husband — he refused to participate in her fears about the biopsy — and next her attempts to come to terms with her own mortality. These conflicts derived from the uncertainty of death and disfigurement, but the next day's good or bad fortune was not the point. The story would end before the operation. My character would find for a moment the place in her mind in which tomorrow's events would cease to matter."

Regardless of how close you are to your material, you still need the ability and will to transform the real events as Solwitz did. She naturally distanced herself from the trauma of the possible breast cancer by placing it in the background of the story, making it merely a catalyst for other psychological concerns.

Still, Solwitz needed to transform the story even further, to keep it from being simply a static psychological portrait. As she points out, "For most stories to be interesting something has to happen, and most often that something must be an act performed by the protagonist. Otherwise we're left with the victim story. In my story my character, who happens to live by a ball park and so do I, starts yelling at a guy who takes a whiz just under her window. In the end, overwrought by etc. etc., she insults the manhood of another fellow who's urinating on her building, and he comes back in his car and starts ramming one of the posts that holds up her house. That has happened to our house, but only accidentally. Then, in an act of solidarity, to save their home, she and her husband throw their television set out the window onto his car. That event was entirely imaginary. It came as a result of following closely the logic of the story. The Cubs are playing that night. Her husband's a fan and more involved it seems with the game on TV than with her panic. She has some odd superstition that if the Cubs lose it means they'll find cancer tomorrow. The use of the TV as a weapon against the guy who wants to demolish her house is plausible psychologically because we've been watching her grow more and more hysterical. It also means that her husband has relinquished his attitude of indifference (in the form of his interest in the ball game) and she of her superstition. While the game goes on outside the window, she and her husband listen on the radio and make love, transcending for the moment at least, the vagaries of mortality."

Basing a story on an actual traumatic event takes a certain quality that not everyone possesses — the ability to see oneself as an abstraction, as yet another character within a larger story. I'm not sure this is a completely positive attribute, perhaps it's even slightly sociopathic. Often, we hear about teenagers, children really, who are able to kill someone without remorse because they don't view the other as completely real. Perhaps writers suffer from this same kind of solipsism and arrested development.

Of course, I'm only half serious here, and in fact, I prefer to view such writers in an opposite light. I'd rather view the writer who faces her own life head-on as courageous rather than cold-blooded.

FAMILY STORIES

The best stories sometimes are the stories you already own, the stories that are part of your life, family stories. Remember Aunt Imelda, who was a gangster's moll during Prohibition? She never married, became a grade school art teacher in Teaneck, New Jersey, and always seemed crabby when you were a kid. She seemed like the last person you'd imagine hanging out with gangsters. Think there's a story there? Or the time Aunt Imelda and your grand-mother were sitting in the dinette drinking coffee and eating lady fingers while you were in your grandmother's bedroom going through a box of old letters. (Your grandmother said you could have the old stamps on the envelopes.) A check slid out, and you looked at it. It was for fifty dollars and it was made out to your grandmother from Aunt Imelda. It was dated 1934 and was uncan-celled! You ran out to the dinette to tell your grandmother of her good fortune, but when you showed it to the two women, they exchanged dark looks, and your grandmother scolded you for tak-ing things that didn't belong to you.

There's definitely a story *there*.

Novelist Bret Lott says family stories "are the stories that have been around forever. You don't go to your family and say, 'Hey, anybody know any good stories I can write about?' The stories that were inside my novel *Jewel* were stories that I had heard growing up. I was never thinking, 'Oh gosh, I'm going to be a novelist. Keep telling me these stories. I want to write about them someday.'

"Many people might look at my family as boring. My dad was a salesman. My mom was a homemaker. It depends how closely you're willing to look. Every family has stories."

When we write about our families, we often base our stories on events that happened to us as well as the other members of our family. In these cases, the writer has as much "ownership" of the event as anyone else. But to use a word like "ownership" is mislead-ing. You can't copyright experience.

As with any other life-based fiction, just because you base a story on Aunt Imelda's life doesn't mean you're restricted to the facts. But, at the same time, whoever your Aunt Imelda is, you must know who she is inside out.

When you research a family story, you may learn something you weren't prepared to learn, and yet, if you're open-minded, these unexpected revelations can become integral to your book or story. With Bret Lott, he learned something unexpected about his grand-mother on a visit just prior to beginning *Jewel*: "Before I started to write the book, I wanted to spend one final time with my grandma. You hear stories about your family. They're huge stories, but if you're going to write the story of your family, you also need to know the mundane, boring details of life. So I spent several days just talking to her at her house. I had a notebook and I was asking her seemingly stupid questions like 'In Mississippi in the 1940s, what did you eat in the wintertime? What was the first car you had? What was your favorite dress?' Detail-oriented questions that would lend authenticity to the story. Then all of a sudden my grandmother stopped and said, 'Oh, I've got to tell you this story.' She told about how she had six children and one day her husband Leston said, 'Let's all go out for a picnic on the lake.' They went out there and they rented a canoe and they took the kids out and let the kids ride around in the canoe and then he said, 'Hey, let's you and me go for a canoe ride.' They climbed into the canoe and he paddled out to the far end of the lake into the . . . 'bullrushes,' was the word she kept saying. 'He jammed it right up in the bullrushes.' Then they made love out there in the canoe. I was sitting in my grandma's kitchen with little lace doilies around, and pictures of the grandkids on the refrigerator, and I was thinking, Grandma, don't tell me this! I don't want to see you and Grandpa . . . So I kind of shrugged it off and thought Oooh yeee! But once I got into the book, once I committed myself to telling the truth of the story, the truth of the novel (there's a difference between my character Jewel and my grandmother), once I got into the life of Jewel, I thought this was something that had to be accounted for. It revealed much about her character, not that she wanted sex, but that it wove its way into the idea of her submitting to him so that she could finally exert her will over him."

Family stories can be difficult to write, in part because of the emotions such material stirs in the author, in part because of the problems such a story might cause if family members read it. Not every family member will be as forthcoming as Bret Lott's grandmother.

If you want to write a family story, the best place to start off might be with your family legends or your black sheep. Who were the strong characters, the ones who were legendarily brave or legendarily cowardly? Who are the ones the family still talks about fifty years after their passing? In my family's case, it's my great-grandmother Hannah, a woman who died years before I was born, but whom I heard about all through my childhood. She was born on a farm in Lithuania. Her mother died in childbirth, and supposedly Hannah was suckled by a she-goat! She fled the farm when her stepmother and father wanted to marry her off to some rich fellow, and she made her way to England, where she had a brother. She worked in a sweatshop, then joined the Yiddish theater and traveled around Europe. She met my great-grandfather in Holland, where he was a shoemaker and supposedly made shoes for the royal family. (Legends, like fiction, don't necessarily have to be true—who knows the truth in all this?) They fell in love, married, had a child, then moved to America. According to my mother, Hannah was, in her youth, a red-haired beauty, and was always very vain, but a great storyteller. She was also the first person in our family to fly in an airplane. This was in the thirties, and she was already elderly and had a heart condition. Everyone begged her not to go, but she insisted. She wanted to fly from New York to Cleveland, where another brother was getting married. She bought a white flying outfit for the occasion. The trip was turbulent but Hannah was calm, and upon landing she was mobbed by reporters—she turned out to be the oldest person at that time to fly in a plane. In those days, you didn't have to actually fly a plane to become famous for flying. Amelia Earhart initially became famous for simply being the first female *passenger* on a trans-Atlantic flight.

This is a bare-boned portrait of my great-grandmother Hannah. I still lack the details and the focus of the story. If you want to write such a story, recall someone in your own family, and try to evoke everything you remember about this person. Write down these memories, and then ask yourself questions. Which of these stories most intrigues you? That's a good place to start. Where's the conflict? When will the story be set, now or in the past? If you set the story in the present, avoid the stock situation of a grandpa or grandma telling a story of the olden days to the younguns on the porch—unless you do something new with the form. That kind of story is older and more tired than grandpa himself.

Of course, if you can twist this idea around and make it fresh, you might succeed, as Richard Spilman does in a powerful story called "The Old Man Tells His Story and Gets It Wrong." With a title like that, you can tell it isn't going to be your average grandpa-in-the-rocker tale. In this story, the protagonist is an old man who tells his grandson an old war tale that he's told a million times. But as he tells it, something goes wrong. The story starts to get away from him, to go in unfamiliar directions and take on a life of its own. Instead of ending as the victor this time, he's cast as the victim.

> Fiercely, then, the wounds began to hurt, and the pain brought back his sight. He lay among the white and yellow flowers staring up at the treetops, which seemed to be on fire. The soldiers were arguing in accents he remembered from his childhood, pointing to him and to the town. One was wiping his bayonet with a fistful of grass. An enemy officer stepped out from the trees and snapped an order.

This might sound like "The Twilight Zone," but it's not. Spilman justifies all this brilliantly by letting us know quite strongly that this anecdote gone haywire is a symptom of a deep and profound physical and psychological change happening to the old man.

It's best to simply set the story in the past and cut out any character based on yourself—that is, the listener. But you must do certain things to make this direct method work well. Often, such a story involves some kind of research (a topic we'll deal with more extensively in a later chapter), such as interviewing any and all relatives who knew your great-grandmother Hannah and the times in which she lived.

You also should ask yourself if the time frame is important. Is this a story that could only have happened in Depression-era Mississippi, or is it timeless? Is it a story that could take place now? If your answer is yes to the second question, you don't need to set it in the past. Setting the story in the present might ultimately free you in your handling of the material, might make the story less biography and more fiction.

Point of view is important here as well. Often, a point of view will automatically suggest itself. You might think, *There's no other logical choice but to tell this story from the point of view of Hannah.* It depends on where the heart of your story is, where the emotional impact lies, and whose character goes through the most profound change. But if one point of view doesn't work, try another. Try multiple viewpoints if you like, but only if it strengthens the reader's understanding of the characters involved. Often, multiple viewpoints, if handled clumsily, have the opposite effect — confusing the reader and giving him a shallow understanding of several characters rather than a deep understanding of one.

You also must be open-minded and willing to change actual events to imagined ones. In my case, I might focus on Hannah's airplane ride, but the relationship I'd see as most important would be with the brother in Cleveland who's getting married. I'd probably make their relationship somewhat ambiguous, even troubled. I'd combine him with the brother in England. I'd ask myself why and how he left the farm in Lithuania first. Is Hannah going to Cleveland now to celebrate her brother or celebrate her own fierce determination and stubbornness? And I don't know if she'd even make it. You see, I'd be willing to kill off my own great-grandmother for the sake of a good story.

CHILDHOOD STORIES

Childhood is not the sole domain of younger writers, but younger writers often look toward childhood for their source material for the simple reason that they remember it vividly, with all its attendant frustrations and misunderstandings. Childhood is the perfect brew pot for fiction. Of course, childhood stories are not necessarily autobiographical. Still, while I've never done scientific study on the matter, I'd bet that autobiography plays a more significant role in this type of story than in any other kind.

One common characteristic of stories told from a child's point of view (which isn't always the case in a childhood story) is an overlay of *dramatic irony*. This kind of irony is unintentional on the part of the main character, as opposed to a more intentional kind of irony like *sarcasm*. Children are naive, often not able to comprehend what's going on around them, and the crafty writer is able to exploit this naiveté. An example might be something like this:

> Mom says that after I take my bath we've got to keep the bathroom door closed or I'll catch a giraffe. I start crying when she rubs me with the towel. I want to catch a giraffe! "Where's the giraffe?" I say.
> "Outside," she says.
> By the time she's done, the giraffe is gone.

Many childhood stories share the ironic overlay of the naive main character. Through the misconceptions of the child character, they make perceptive comments on the crazy world of adults. Likewise, the collision between the child's world and the adult world often produces a welling of emotion in the reader that would not be possible if told from an adult's point of view. Isaak Babel's "The Story of My Dovecot," for example, is about a boy in Russia at the turn of the century who keeps doves as pets. However, on the day he buys two new doves (as a reward for doing well on his school exams), he's caught in the midst of a pogrom. The character has no understanding of what's going on around him or why, and that makes the story all the more tragic:

> He dealt me a flying blow with the hand that was clutching the bird. Kate's wadded back seemed to turn upside down, and I fell to the ground in my new overcoat.
>
> "Their spawn must be wiped out," said Kate, straightening up over the bonnets. "I can't a-bear their spawn, nor their stinking menfolk."
>
> She said more things about our spawn, but I heard nothing of it. I lay on the ground, and the guts of the crushed bird trickled down from my temple. They flowed down my cheek, winding this way and that, splashing, blinding me. The tender pigeon-guts slid down over my forehead, and I closed my solitary unstopped-up eye so as not to see the world that spread out before me. This world was tiny, and it was awful. A stone lay just before my eyes, a little stone so chipped as to resemble the face of an old woman with a large jaw. A piece of string lay not far away, and a bunch of feathers that still breathed. My world was tiny, and it was awful. I closed my eyes so as not to see it, and pressed myself tight into the ground that lay beneath me in soothing dumbness. This trampled earth in no way resembled real life, waiting for exams in real life.

But it does unfortunately resemble real life.

These stories also are all coming-of-age stories. Such stories focus on a young narrator, naive by definition, who begins the story wet around the ears, understanding little of the world, and ends up through her experiences making the rite of passage from childhood into adulthood. See, for instance, James Joyce's classic story, "Araby," about the self-delusions and disappointments of a young boy's infatuation with an older girl.

It's hard to write a childhood story that isn't a coming-of-age story. Almost all stories involve some kind of character change, and one of the most profound changes of life is the transition from child to adult. This presents the greatest challenge in writing childhood stories: Since they are almost invariably coming-of-age stories and since so many are written, how can we write one that's different from the rest? It's a challenge but it's by no means impossible. Success rests in the telling of the story, how fresh the perceptions of the narrator are, how unusual the story is, and, most important, whether the ending can avoid feeling pat, inevitable in its coming-of-ageness.

However, editors, by and large, have a bias against child narrators. This bias is not universal, but it exists primarily because magazines are inundated with such stories. Be aware of this bias, but don't let it dissuade you from writing a story based on your childhood experiences. It's just an extra hurdle to jump.

I was always doing things as a kid that I've been trying to fit into my fiction ever since. Like the time I organized a pickpocket ring at Atlantic Beach Day Camp in New York. One time, someone brought some rabbits to class in first grade, and the teacher said we could have a rabbit if we got a note from our parents. I knew that my mother wouldn't allow me to have a rabbit, so I went home and forged a note that read:

> Robin can hav rabbi
> sined Mom

Another time I invited my first grade teacher for dinner because I had a crush on her. She said she'd be delighted, and asked me what time to show up.

"Nine," I said. Nine was actually my bedtime. I suppose I imagined my mother saying, "Well, we've already eaten, but this is Robin's bedtime. So if you want to sleep over you can."

When I arrived home that evening, I forgot all about my teacher. She showed up at nine sharp and rang the doorbell.

"Robin, go see who that is," said my mother.

"No," I said.

"Come on," she said. "Go see who it is. Tell them I'll be down in a minute."

I went downstairs, looked through the window, and saw my teacher dressed up with a fur collar and her hair made up. She saw me and waved. I waved back and ran upstairs.

"Who is it?" my mother asked.

"Nobody."

My mother shook her head and walked downstairs to see for herself. I tagged behind her saying, "She wants to eat. Don't let her in."

I've twice tried to include this anecdote in a story. The first time the editor who saw it suggested I cut it out. It was funny, she said, but it had little bearing on the story as a whole. So I cut it. Recently, I put the same anecdote in another story and another editor had the same problem with it. This time, however, I didn't cut the anecdote. In this story, I think it does have bearing on the story as a whole. Who knows? I might be wrong. Perhaps I'm too fond of the episode, and before the story makes it into my next collection of stories, I'm going to give it a hard look and decide whether to axe it again or not. I can always save it for yet another story.

The way I related the above anecdote is important, too. There are countless ways to describe an actual event, whether from childhood or not, depending on who the writer is, or even the mood of the writer as he sits down to put pen to paper, or neurons to VDT, as the case may be. I've told that story so many times I've almost got it memorized. Still, is that the way things actually happened? No. That sequence of events happened, but it's still fictionalized. Words shape the way we view an event, and they can never truly transfer the full experience to the reader, no matter how accurate the writer tries to be. Accuracy, in this context, at least, should not even be the writer's aim.

If you use something from your childhood in a story, an anecdote like the one above, or if you base an entire story on your childhood, there are a few things to look out for:

1. Don't romanticize childhood. While children are naive, they're not necessarily innocent. Children can be much more brutal and

frank than adults, and often adults' golden memories of childhood are little more than wishful thinking.

2. Avoid precious kid talk. Often, what seems cute or funny in real life might fall completely flat in a short story, seeming too heavy-handed.

3. Inevitably, someone will criticize your story, especially if it's written in the first person, on the grounds that "a child wouldn't sound like that." If you *were* completely accurate, you wouldn't have much of a story there. It would be about eight lines, written on wide-ruled paper with a fat pencil. Have you ever heard a child tell a story? In *Mollie Is Three, Growing Up in School* (University of Chicago Press), by Vivian Gussin Paley, the author recorded much of the play-acting and storytelling of her class of three-year-olds:

> Most first stories . . . lie somewhere between the compulsory and the accidental. They refer to scenes that are not overwhelming but need to be played out again. Mollie's first story, for example, dealt with the bad guys she heard about in school.
> "About a bad guy and a horse. The robbers and the horse. He takes things away from the girl."
> Here are some other first stories dictated by this year's three-year-olds:
> "Batman goes whoosh. In the Batmobile" (Barney).
> "The gorilla gets out of the cage" (William).
> "The mommy walks and eats and takes a nappie" (Stuart).
> "Me finds a train. And the train stopped. And the trains sleeped" (Edward).
> "Five kitty cats run away. Superman pows them away" (Sybil).

As we discussed earlier, a short story, or a novel for that matter, is artifice. You want the story to seem real, to suspend the reader's disbelief, but if the story is any good, it will never be a completely accurate account. A completely accurate account would ricochet from one subject to another with hardly any logical progression.

That's how children's minds work. They are highly associative creatures.

Your way out is to either write the story in first person, past tense, or in third person. With first person, past tense, there's almost an invisible narrator behind the child narrator. In other words, it's assumed that the narrator is looking back from an adult vantage point and telling the story, though it's not necessary to know exactly how old the adult narrator is. With third person, you have that same kind of removal between the child and the narrator. But even if you want to write a story from a child's point of view in first person, present tense, go ahead. Just steel yourself for the inevitable criticism.

Of course, not all of that criticism is invalid. You wouldn't normally have a five-year-old talking about, for instance, dysfunction in the contemporary American family — unless, of course, you used the narrator's advanced vocabulary in an ironic way as Frank O'Connor does in his story, "My Oedipus Complex." The story is about a five-year-old boy who has his mother all to himself while his father is away in the army during World War I. His father makes rare appearances like Santa Claus, which suits the boy just fine, until one day, the war ends.

> One morning, I got into the big bed, and there, sure enough, was Father in his usual Santa Claus manner, but later, instead of a uniform, he put on his best blue suit, and Mother was as pleased as anything. I saw nothing to be pleased about, because, out of uniform, Father was altogether less interesting, but she only beamed, and explained that our prayers had been answered, and off we went to Mass to thank God for having brought Father safely home.
>
> The irony of it! That very day when he came in to dinner he took off his boots and put on his slippers, donned the dirty old cap he wore about the house to save him from colds, crossed his legs, and began to talk gravely to Mother, who looked anxious. Naturally, I disliked her looking anxious, because it destroyed her good looks, so I interrupted him.
>
> "Just a moment, Larry!" she said gently.

This was only what she said when we had boring visitors, so I attached no importance to it and went on talking.

Young writers sometimes have a difficult time finding subject matter from real life, and that's why childhood is often a good source for their stories. Not long ago, a student of mine, Courtney, wrote a pastiche of loosely connected anecdotes that she undoubtedly knocked out the night before the story was due. When we talked about the story in class, the other students felt disconnected from the narrative because it lacked any sense of structure. But there was one scene they all responded to, a scene about the parents of the narrator being chili cook-off fanatics and dragging their two kids to chili cook-offs around the country. "That's my parents," the author piped in. "They're crazy about chili. That's all they think about. My dad was the Texas chili cook-off champion last year."

Now we were interested and asked Courtney about the world of chili cook-offs. Among other things, we learned about cow bingo, a game played at many chili cook-offs in which a huge bingo card is chalked in the grass, people bet on a number, and then a cow is made to wander over the card. Wherever the animal drops a cow pie, that's the number that wins.

Soon Courtney embarked upon an epic tale of two fanatical chili cooks and their somewhat disenchanted daughter and son. The story ended up being twenty-seven pages long, and this in an intro to creative writing class in which most students think that they've written a novel if they go beyond five pages. Admittedly, the story needed some cutting, but Courtney was engaged with the material. "I can't believe it," she lamented to me one day. "I went away to school to get away from chili cook-offs, and now I'm writing about them."

TELL-IT-LIKE-IT-IS STORIES

On occasion, a writer will write a story pretty much as it happened in real life, but this is a rarity. There are no rules or directions for writing such a story, only that, again, you should be sure you don't confuse a good anecdote for a good story. But sometimes an occurrence in life will imitate the arc of a story and all you have to do is write it down and change a few details here and there.

Sometimes you'll know the tell-it-like-it-is story when it happens to you. It won't happen often, but all of a sudden you'll find yourself in a situation that you know immediately is a story. It's a strange feeling when it happens. Regardless of your religious beliefs, you'll think about fate, kismet, karma, whatever. But beware. The ironies of life can be much more heavy-handed than those in fiction.

Josip Novakovich was able to write a story pretty much as it happened, about the death of his father. It's a story called "The Apple," first published in *Ploughshares*. He says that the material was difficult for him, that before this story he was able to write about all else in his life but this event. And when he was finally able to write the story, he wasn't sure whether to call it memoir or fiction, but decided on fiction. He had, after all, changed some of the details and shifted a couple of events around in time. But, as mentioned earlier, even memoirists often do this.

> My father looked very healthy on the day of his death. There was radiance in his face, light in his eyes, his cheeks were ruddy with a good circulation of blood.
>
> It was December 6th, and there was a slanted snow-storm outdoors. When you looked through the window, you had a feeling that the whole house was being ascended into heaven sideways. The patches of snow that fell were big, like the down of a huge celestial bird, whose one wing covered our whole valley, and the wing must have been flapping, because it was windy. As soon as the snow touched the ground, it melted.

In real life, Novakovich's father died in February, and it wasn't snowing, but snow, he says, felt right for the story. This doesn't matter. A few details may be changed, but the core of the experience is essentially honest, and that's what's important. As proof of that fact, when his older brother read the story, he took it as a family document, a testament, and locked it in a vault with other important family papers.

Since writing "The Apple," Novakovich has written an essay with his father in it, but in this he focuses more on the man's religious fervor toward the end of his life, and the death plays a background role.

So is this cheating in some way, calling something fiction that's factually based? Not at all. But some writers act sheepish about writing this kind of story, and they are reluctant to admit this is what they've done, as though we might think less of them, as though they're somehow lazy for writing something so factual. That's non-sense, of course. The details you choose, the words you choose, the ordering of events — all of these take an act of the imagination and some skill as a writer. In some ways, writing such a story is more difficult than writing a story whole cloth from your imagination. Even in the most factually based stories, you need to know what memories to leave out and what to build up or exaggerate. If you're absolutely true in every respect to what happened, you'll probably wind up with a disjointed jumble with vague and flat images. The story must ultimately seem of a piece, to achieve what Edgar Allen Poe called *unity of effect*. This unity of effect is perhaps more difficult to achieve in a completely or nearly autobiographical story, because a memory that seems crucial to the writer might completely baffle the reader and seem extraneous to the story. It takes practice to be able to decide which of these memories *really* fit in and which seem important only because the writer wants them to be impor-tant, because they happened. The best measure of your success or failure in writing such an autobiographical piece is the cool eye of an honest critic. If someone you respect suggests that something autobiographical doesn't fit your story, listen to her and make those cuts, as painful as they might be.

Madison Smartt Bell was just out of college when he wrote "The Lie Detector" and "The Forgotten Bridge," two stories in his cele-brated collection *Zero db and Other Stories* (Ticknor and Fields). Both stories are told from the first person by a narrator of whom we know very little, except that he's a young white male trying his best to survive in and around New York City. "The Forgotten Bridge" takes place in a run-down tenement in the Williamsburg section of Brooklyn and deals with the narrator's friendships with the other people in the building, most notably a young Hispanic man called Pollo and his friend Angel. Friendship is perhaps too strong a word — more like a guarded acquaintanceship, at least on the narra-tor's part. "The Lie Detector," a story that was reprinted in *The Best American Short Stories of 1987*, deals with the same narrator, maybe six months or so earlier in his life. In this story, he's being evicted from his apartment in Hoboken because his landlord has sold the building. The landlord refuses to return his rent deposit, and in the meantime, his new landlord and/or the super of the building (the narrator isn't sure which one) tries to shake him down for an extra hundred dollars. On top of this, the narrator is practically starving and searching for any kind of work he can find. At one point, he must take a lie detector test to secure a job.

Bell says that both stories were fairly accurate accounts of his life at the time, and except for changing the names, the characters were all real people. "The Lie Detector" was too long, he felt, so he cut about ten pages as he was drafting it. Regardless, even if everything happened in these stories exactly as they're laid out, they're still fictional stories. The narration is purposely distant and oblique:

> I took the form to a chair and looked it over, and it was asking a lot of questions I really couldn't afford to answer. I hadn't expected anything like it. I had expected to be asked about drug addiction and felony convictions, two problems I happened not to have, and here were all these questions about problems that I did have. But I was up there already so I decided to try it. I filled out the form with what I wished was the truth and waited for them to call me. I sat there hoping that polygraph tests really are as unreliable as statistics say they are.

Makes you curious, doesn't it? It's supposed to. That's *indirection*. We never learn what those problems are, what the narrator hopes won't be uncovered about himself. Why? If the narrator doesn't want the lie detector to uncover these problems, he's certainly not going to tell us about them. That, in itself, gives the narration some of its ironic tension and makes it fiction — no matter *how* fact-based the story is.

We learn only through inference about the narrator's feelings and beliefs, and though he's supposedly telling us about the lives of other people, by the end of each story, we have a fairly clear portrait of his own moral state, in part because of what he says, in part because of what he leaves out. This method of indirection will automatically pull you back from a story that really happened to you, will give you the requisite distance to create a fictional treatment of real events. That can hardly be stressed enough. When you write a story of this kind, allow your narrator to withhold certain information. Allow him to be a little cagey, a little less than forthcoming about his own weaknesses and gray areas—just as long as the reader sees through such subterfuge. Of course, these weaknesses might well be your own weaknesses, but remember what Faulkner said about the human heart in conflict with itself. Remember also that you have the perfect defense. It's only a story, you can always say.

JOBS AND OTHER TRUE EXPERIENCES

I admit I've done some things in my life just for the experience, so that I might write about them later. But the truth is, most of what I consciously experienced so I could write about it later didn't pan out. I never wrote about these experiences, and I probably never will (at least as fiction). One summer I was a gravedigger's apprentice. I wasn't a very good gravedigger's apprentice, and I didn't last long, but that's what I did the summer I was eighteen. The foreman was a guy named Wilbur who wore a back brace and who said he was going to retire soon. He said the cemetery was going to give him his own plot when he retired, which, he said, was better than some businessman's watch because it would last longer. My older brother, Jonathan, worked with me, and Wilbur called him Big Jon and me Little Jon because he didn't think Robin was a proper name for a boy to have. It seems that the seminal experience in Wilbur's life had been his time during World War II in Gibraltar, because just about all he talked about while Jonny and I toiled in the sun was those "hot-blooded Gibraltar gals."

Even at eighteen, I wanted to be a writer, though I was probably more interested in being a writer than in actually writing. Still, as Wilbur talked, I kept thinking, *This is going to make a great story.* It didn't, or at least it hasn't yet. I don't think this is due to any kind of moral quandary. It's not because of my mercenary approach to the experience, the fact that I wanted to write about Wilbur and the whole graveyard crowd from the outset. No, it's probably more simply that I haven't gotten around to writing the story yet. I've lived through a number of experiences during which I thought, *I'll probably write about this someday,* and I did. Or even more likely, the answer is that what struck me as fascinating material at the age of eighteen no longer seems all that striking now that I'm in my thirties.

One summer during graduate school in Iowa, a friend asked me if I'd like to pick up some extra money as a bartender. He said a friend of his was opening a bar and needed some help. It turned out this bar was Iowa City's first and only strip joint (actually, it was right over the city line), called Taboo's.

I jumped at the chance, not because I was an aficionado of strip joints, but because it seemed like a strange thing to do. *At the very least,* I thought, *it'll make a good story.* From gravedigger's apprentice to bartender in a strip joint. I'm not sure that was a step up.

In any case, Taboo's was a strange place in more than one way. It was located in the clubhouse on a golf course, so the decor was not your typical strip joint fare. It had a big old hearth on one side of the room and a mantle lined with trophies of gold men swinging clubs. In the middle of the room was the platform on which the strippers did their acts.

The strippers were pretty interesting, too. The most popular one was a woman named Brandy (they all seemed to be named after alcoholic beverages) who did a rug act that people came from far and wide to see. There was also a minister's daughter (you see, if I wrote that in a story, you'd think, 'Right, a minister's daughter') whose name I forget. Her boyfriend had never seen her strip and used to drop her off and then pick her up when she was finished. She danced very stiffly, as though removing layer after layer of flannel underwear. There was also a woman we nicknamed Miss Dubuque (she'd won some title like that) who absolutely loathed the audience. She danced with complete hatred in her eyes. She didn't even try to hide it, which did not make her the most popular stripper, and I don't think I ever saw a man dare stick any folding money in her G-string.

The most pathetic of all the dancers was a woman who had at one time been a stripper in Las Vegas and had owned $7,000 worth of costumes. Three weeks before she came to work at Taboo's, she and her husband had ceremoniously burned all her old costumes, thinking she'd never have to strip again. But a week later, her husband was unexpectedly laid off from his job. So now she'd gone back to her degrading work at Taboo's. The woman also had a large hysterectomy scar. I talked to her a lot at the bar and felt sorry for her, knowing she wasn't going to last long, knowing she didn't want to last long. When she danced, the men in the bar looked away, scars being something they were trying to escape from in their own lives.

It wasn't long after that I quit, realizing that what I thought of as story material was much more important than that.

But my favorite time at Taboo's was ladies' night. On this night, male strippers danced at the club, and they were much better and seemed to enjoy themselves more than the women who danced. The men dressed up in campy costumes like sailor uniforms and tails and tuxes and seemed to glory in the attention from the overwhelmingly female clientele, mostly young women who worked at the phone company. These women, in their adulation of the male strippers, acted twice as abandoned as the male clientele on a normal night. The women hooted and danced, but the men just looked slack-jawed and slobbered over themselves between gulps of beer. So I enjoyed ladies' night. I also enjoyed it because sometimes a hapless man, unaware that it was ladies' night, would wander in from the race track, farm or university, and a look of horror would overcome him when he glanced at the stage. But he'd paid his cover, so he'd belly up to the bar, clutch it till his knuckles turned white and refuse to look over his shoulder at the stage, afraid he might turn into a pillar of salt or someone might think he actually *liked* to see guys take their clothes off! The irony, of course, was that the female strippers were not available to him and his kind, but if he'd been a little less homophobic, he might have had some luck with the hooting operators there for ladies' night. Or maybe not.

So, if I wrote a story about this, where would I go with it? If I told it from a point of view based on my own, I'd say it would make a pretty obvious coming-of-age story. Or I could focus on the woman with the hysterectomy. She's much more interesting to me than I am. Still, you have to avoid the obvious ironies. Don't end such a story with the poor woman dancing on the stage and the men looking away from her scar. Avoid writing your typical down-on-your-luck-isn't-life-tragic, aren't-men-pigs story. For that matter, avoid writing *anything* typical. The successful fiction writer is not the one who reinforces our old notions of life. Actually, that's not completely true. Many monetarily successful fiction writers reinforce stale ideas and recycle plots and characters. But if you're aiming for those old eternal verities, you need to show us the world in a new light. You need to recast those verities through the rich and varied details that you have experienced and observed.

And, as we've discussed earlier, the characters, not the events, should take center stage in your story. Find out which character intrigues you the most and try writing the story about him or her. Depending on the point of view, what happens in the story will change considerably. What if you told the story from Miss Dubuque's point of view? Kind of lame, I think.

> The pigs, Miss Dubuque thinks, as she twists and turns and moans on the floor. You think you're in control, but I am in control, not you. Swine!

If you tell it from the point of view based on me, here's what it might look like:

> My friend, Will, asked me if I'd like to pick up some extra money that summer. I said, "Sure, doing what?"
> "Bartending," he replied with a sheepish grin.
> "Dang!" I said. "When do I begin?" Little did I expect where I would be tending bar!

Yawn.

Or you could tell it from the minister's daughter's point of view, but that seems so pointed, no one would believe you. "But it really happened," you'd say. So what?

How about her boyfriend's point of view? Maybe, but I keep coming back to that woman with the hysterectomy. Obviously, if you're unsubtle and approach the story like a mongrel with a bone in its mouth, you could destroy this one, too, by making the irony as heavy-handed as the previous examples. But there's still something emotionally interesting about this woman to me. In the words of Sherwood Anderson, "Something must be understood."

Still, if I were to write this story, I might take it out of the strip joint, at least partly, and focus on some other, less sensationalistic aspect of the woman's life. This is a strategy writers often use when dealing with autobiographical material. The notes fit together slowly, picked up from different stages of life. I might combine this tale of the Iowa City stripper with another story from my life. For instance, a friend once told me of visiting a farm in Iowa, a farm that was run by a young couple she had just met. They proudly walked her through the fields and showed her their livestock and produce. Originally, they had lived somewhere urban and were relatively new to this life. What my friend remembered most, however, was the kitchen, in which hung full strings of peppers and garlic and fresh herbs. The next day, this couple was killed in an auto accident, and my friend was haunted by the image of their kitchen, so well stocked with all these vegetables and herbs. That image, for some reason, has stayed with me, too.

What if you combined the story of the stripper with the hysterectomy and the tale of the young farm couple? Certainly, a farming stripper with a hysterectomy would be a slightly different take on things. Phrased like that, it sounds ridiculous. But if you're going to write, you must take risks, and the biggest risk is that you may look like a fool. For the sake of argument, can you see anything that might connect the two anecdotes—in terms of character, theme, plot? Again, that's what writers do when patching together episodes from life. They make *associations*. Often these associations are thematic. Sometimes we're not sure *what* they are or why our minds have made these strange connections between events separated by time and distance. Your job in the story is to find out exactly how they're connected. That might seem like an odd strategy. How can you write a story if you don't know what it's about? Writing is a discovery process, as much for the writer as for the reader.

How about this? I keep going back to the notion that this woman and her husband had burned her costumes just weeks before she was forced back to work as a stripper. At that moment, they must have thought they had life beat, or maybe it was a rash gesture, something defiant in the face of defeat. And the hysterectomy, of course, meant that she couldn't have any children, yet here they were surrounded by the fecundity of their farm. To me, there's something worth exploring there.

Sometimes this strategy of combining two seemingly unrelated incidents doesn't pan out. The main danger is a lack of focus, but if you've already completely figured out what your story is about before you've begun, your insights probably won't be that startling.

In any case, a true-experience story can be limiting if you stick to the real events of what happened to you. Ask yourself what the point is of relating your true experience. Because it was bizarre? Because it was a wacky job training spider monkeys to dance the hula at Mondo Monkey World in Ft. Lauderdale the summer you turned seventeen? Remember what we've said about anecdotes. One reason that such stories often don't work is because they hinge on the anecdotal. What should concern you first and foremost are the nuances of character in your story. And that character might not be you at all.

STORIES FROM THE NEWSPAPER

As we've discussed, the fact that you've lived through something can actually get in your way, can make it difficult for you to tackle the material. That's why you need distance and why it's often much easier to write about someone else. Newspapers are full of potential story material.

A few years ago, Dan Rather was accosted on the streets of New York by thugs who pushed him to the ground, kicked him and shouted, "What is the frequency, Kenneth?" The story made all the papers, but of course, no one, least of all Dan Rather, knew what his attackers were talking about. The story was a little absurd and intriguing, but only intriguing because of the dramatic questions involved: Who is Kenneth? What is this talk of frequencies? It was also intriguing because it happened to Dan Rather. If it had happened to you or me, no one would have been interested — or not many people, at least. I asked my writing students to do an in-class exercise with this incident as the basis for a scene, and predictably, the scenes they came up with weren't all that interesting. It was my miscalculation. I hadn't thought the assignment through. After all, where could one go with such a silly idea? The results were one-note stories in which Dan Rather turned out to be a Russian spy. Often, the mystery of an event is much more interesting than any solution one can come up with.

A couple of years later, a Russian circus was stranded outside of Atlanta, Georgia, when their Arab backers deserted them. They spent weeks in a motel: the acrobats, the sword swallowers, the clowns. Something about that news story seemed evocative to me. I could see an entire novel about a Russian circus stranded in the American South. I suppose the reason this seems so intriguing is that the situation has larger societal implications than, say, the Dan Rather story. I'm not quite sure what those implications are, but that's, in part, what I'd try to discover if I were going to write a novel about this situation. Also, I have lived in the South, not too far from Atlanta, so there's probably some chord in me the story touches. That's an important point. Even if the story has nothing to do with you on an obvious level, it most likely has something important to do with you on a subconscious level, or else you wouldn't be interested in the idea in the first place.

A lot of other people, millions perhaps, saw that Russian circus story. How many of those millions were writers? Let's say two thousand. And of those two thousand, how many thought the idea might make an interesting short story or novel? Maybe fifty. And of those fifty, how many do you think will actually start writing the story or novel? None, I bet. The point is that a lot people get ideas from the same sources, but few follow through. And even if they do, your novel about a Russian circus stranded outside of Atlanta will be very different from mine. You're not competing against me or any other writer for ideas. You're competing against yourself and your natural tendency to procrastinate and be undisciplined—every writer fights against these twin evils. And then, of course, maybe I don't think it's a good idea to begin with, so why are you trying to second-guess whether I'm going to beat you to the punch and come out with my classic Russian circus novel before you?

As with your own life, you must change and adapt ideas you find in the newspaper. Remember, most of us have probably already read the story, so we don't need a simple retelling. You don't want our reaction to be simply, "Oh, I remember when that happened." Again, you must mold and shape the story, mixing it with your imagination and perhaps events from your own life. Ask yourself what interests you about the material. Maybe you won't completely know the answer to that question, but it should be more than, "Gee, it's terrible when things like that happen." We already know that from the news story.

What often attracts us to a bizarre story in a newspaper is the "what," the odd circumstances of the story. A short story should focus more on the "why" and "who," as *elucidated* by the "what." In other words, the action or events in the story should show us something *about* the characters and their motivations. A car chase in a movie might be exciting because we respond viscerally to visual stimulation. We don't necessarily have to know who the chasers and chasees are. Our adrenaline will naturally start pumping. That's not the case in a short story or novel. Simply describing action devoid of character, no matter how intriguing the action is, will leave readers in the dark unless we know and care about the characters.

Joyce Carol Oates based her story "Where Are You Going, Where Have You Been?" on a newspaper account of a serial rapist/murderer who was roaming the Midwest at the time. But she didn't tell the story from his point of view. She told it from the point of view of one of his victims. The violence is all implied, all off-stage. It's the threat of violence, the inevitability of it, that creates and sustains tension in the story. In the end, as the soon-to-be victim follows the murderer into his car, Oates shows the young girl's terror (and her fate) by describing the vast, anonymous land around her. It's not necessary for Oates to go any further in the story. She doesn't have to describe the violence in detail. Our imaginations can create the scenario. And by implying the violence rather than showing it, she makes the story all the more haunting, one that lingers for years.

Almost any newspaper story can be transformed into a piece of fiction. The main strategy is to focus. And you focus on character, even in stories that deal ostensibly with the largest, most gripping and complex issues in the newspaper today: serial killers, televangelism, Elvis! You must focus on a believable character because if you focus instead on the issue itself, what you've written is an essay, not a story. The issue will overwhelm the characters. Your stories should not have a message in the sense that a sermon has a message: AIDS is terrible and AIDS discrimination is shameful and discrimination against the homeless is shameful, too. Short stories and novels, like real life, are far more ambiguous than sermons. The distinction between right and wrong, good and evil, is often blurred. You don't need to write a story with a message, because most often these messages are ones we hear and acknowledge day after day. We all know that AIDS and homelessness are tragic. We don't need a short story or novel to reinforce that. The first responsibility of a writer is to create believable characters, and the issues, or themes, should arise organically from who the characters are, not from some preconceived notion of what issue you want the story to deal with.

On the other hand, it's quite all right to write a story with a character in it who has AIDS or who is homeless, as long as the story is first and foremost about that character, and AIDS or homelessness is just an aspect of his personality—like the way he parts his hair to the right or has a pet cat. Maybe AIDS and homelessness would have more bearing on the character's personality than a hair part or a pet, but the point is that AIDS and homelessness should not be emblems or symbols, thus transforming the character into a mere symbol or stereotype rather than a complex character.

There *are* artists who handle big issues well. On June 14, 1993, Anna Deavere Smith opened a successful one-woman show, "Twilight: Los Angeles, 1992," based on the Los Angeles riots. Smith did extensive research for her play, interviewing 175 people who were intimately involved with the riots. The critics agreed the play was brilliant. Part of its brilliance undoubtedly derives from Smith's own ability to transform herself into the various roles, from a Korean family to former Los Angeles police chief Daryl Gates to Rodney King's aunt. She uses their words verbatim, captured over nine months with her tape recorder, to bring about these transformations. Notice, though, that while the subject is ostensibly the Los Angeles riots, Smith focuses on character more than event—twenty-four characters in this case, culled from the more than 175 people she interviewed. In her own words, she looks for those "characteristic moments" from her subjects, the moment "when people actually take control of their interview."

That's what any good writer looks for, those characteristic moments when the essence of who the character is seems to be revealed through speech or gesture. In these cases, the characters seem to take control of your story or novel. They speak faster than you can record what they're saying. That's when you know your writing works.

Some people might not consider what Smith has done as a creative achievement at all. As stated earlier, some writers believe that any creative work based on real life represents "a failure of the imagination." Actually, the case is quite the opposite. Any time you can transform real life—and we've seen how difficult that can be—it represents a triumph of the imagination.

But what about the case of Anna Deavere Smith? What's creative about taking the words verbatim out of the mouths of her subjects and saying them on stage? You can say someone's words verbatim, but you're still interpreting them, though perhaps subtly, through gesture and intonation. Smith taped more than 175 interviews and culled these down to twenty-four. She looked for "characteristic moments." If you were doing the production, perhaps you'd find different characteristic moments, or maybe you wouldn't see any at all. In short, Smith ordered real life. And that's something that takes a great deal of imagination and understanding.

A lot of newspaper stories are either amusing or cute or shocking. Not human interest stories, but alien interest. Primate interest. People doing the kinds of outrageous things that work fine in real life, but when you transfer them to a fictional setting people say, "Uh-uh. Won't work. I'm not buying." Go figure.

Here's one that appeared just recently, a story that got a lot of play in the national media. Twenty evangelical Texans, ages one to sixty-three, stripped off all their clothing because they thought it was possessed by the Devil, piled into a 1990 Pontiac Grand Am, and took off through Texas and Louisiana until they finally slammed into a tree. They were more or less fine, but still naked, when the local sheriff disgorged them from the Grand Am. As police officer Doyle Nealy (make a note of that name; it's a good one) observed: "It was just a religious type of thing."

While this kind of newspaper story isn't my kind of material, there *are* writers who use such material as the kernels for their work and end up with stories that are funny and profound. Much depends on the individual writer's sensibilities, and that's why you can't make ironclad rules for writers.

One such writer is Max Childers, whose two novels deal with characters and situations right out of today's headlines. His first novel, *Things Undone* (Wyrick and Co.), is a wicked satire of televangelists. His second novel, *Alpha Omega* (Wyrick and Co.), deals with a paranoid ex-con named Bobby Snipes, who, as the second Elvis, becomes a Messianic figure and main attraction at a theme park in Myrtle Beach called Graceland by the Sea. Childers believes that the more sophisticated the media becomes, "the more information we get, the less we know. I think one of the duties of the novelist is to study what goes on. In this sense, novels are pieces of reportage too. . . . Perhaps if we write well enough, our fiction can lessen the confusion about how we live, make us less duped."

Newspaper stories rarely give you an in-depth portrait of a person, so if you use a newspaper account as the basis of a story, your job is to invent, to expand on our knowledge of the characters, to make them believable. As we discussed in the previous chapter, you do this through salient detail and by trying to come to some understanding of their desires, their motivations for their actions. All actions have motivations, even ones that seem "crazy." Never write about a character whose motivations are unclear to you. If they're unclear to you, they'll be unclear to the reader. That doesn't mean you have to know a character's motivations from the outset. Just as you can come to discover what your story is "about," you can also come to discover who your characters are and what makes them tick. In any case, you want your readers to understand your characters, to feel what they feel, to ultimately be moved by what happens to them. If you don't know why something happens, you can't expect your reader to fully share the experience of your character.

If you find a story that interests you in the newspaper, ask yourself what is in the story that intrigues you so much. Is it the situation, or the characters? Is it both? Let's say you're intrigued by the story about the car of naked evangelical Texans. The situation is interesting, but so are the people. Why would they act in a way that seems bizarre to most of us? It's unlikely that you can write a convincing story shifting from one point of view to the other, so you must choose a central point of view. It could be the preacher. It could be one of the cops. Or perhaps another, less visible (no pun intended) member of the group. I would go for the latter because the preacher seems a little too obvious, too likely to veer into stereotype. And the cop's point of view would be too limited. So you must decide who among that tangled mob would make a good protagonist. The preacher's daughter? Again, too obvious, too much of a stereotype. A child? Maybe, but perhaps too limited again. Often, the first characters who leap to mind in a situation like this will be stereotypes. It wouldn't be easy, but you should probably invent someone who is none of these stereotypes, maybe someone based on an acquaintance of yours, someone you've known in the past who might just wind up nude with nineteen others in a 1990 Grand Am. Or maybe even better, base it on someone you wouldn't expect at *all* to be there. Maybe your mother or father. Make it the story of how she or he wound up in this unlikely situation. In that way you'd mix your memory, your imagination and an objective newspaper account to create something completely new, and something that would really interest us—we'd want to know as much as you how your mother ended up there!

It's usually a little easier to comprehend the motivations of people in newspaper accounts. A recent story in *The New York Times* concerned the skeletons of four Eskimos that the American Museum of Natural History was shipping to Greenland. Apparently, in 1896, explorer Robert E. Peary enticed several Greenland Eskimos to travel to New York with him to be put on display. On October 11, 1897, *The New York Times* reported, "The unfortunate little savages have caught cold or warmth, they do not know which, but assuming it was the latter their sole endeavor yesterday was to keep cool. Their efforts in this direction were a source of amusement to several scores of visitors."

The present-day *Times* reporter, in a tone radically different from his patronizing and cruel predecessor, chronicles this shameful time when we put people on display like animals. Of course, most of the Eskimos died of disease, and the last surviving adult was shipped back to Greenland. That left one child, a boy named Minik, who was blithely handed over for adoption to William Wallace, the superintendent of the museum's building. As the article notes, it was a strange choice, because it was this man who actually bleached the bones of the boy's father and the other dead Eskimos and then handed them over to the museum.

In 1907, an article in *The New York World* appeared, headlined "Give Me My Father's Body," and related Minik's anguish and his frustrated attempts to make the museum relinquish his father's skeleton. By that time, Peary had ceased to have any interest in the boy and was concerned with other, more important things, such as receiving from Teddy Roosevelt a gold medal for his exploration.

In 1909, Minik was sent to Manhattan College to study engineering. That same year, he acquired a press agent, was reported as suicidal and then disappeared. Peary, for his part, was racing to find the North Pole when another article appeared in the *Times* about Minik, in which his press agent claimed that Minik didn't feel any particular warmth for Peary and might in some way scheme to defeat his attempt to find the Pole, though God knows how he would have done that. Still, the explorer's wife took the report seriously enough and decided the best thing to do was to ship Minik off to Greenland. So, once he resurfaced, he was offered a one-way ticket home, an offer he didn't refuse. But before boarding the ship, he gave reporters one more statement:

> You're a race of scientific criminals. I know I'll never get my father's bones out of the American Museum of Natural History. I am glad enough to get away before they grab my brains and stuff them into a jar.

But Minik was wrong. They *had* grabbed his brains. He didn't fare well in Greenland. He didn't know how to hunt or fish, and he didn't speak the language. Slowly, painfully, he learned, but he finally gave up and returned to the United States in 1916. Soon, he wound up as a lumberjack in New Hampshire, a loner who stayed in a shack he built himself. Then, in 1918, he contracted the flu that was epidemic at the time and died at the age of twenty-nine. Now he's buried in a cemetery in Pittsburg, New Hampshire, while his father's bones have finally been shipped back to Greenland for a traditional burial in the Arctic permafrost.

Does this story strike you as potentially fruitful? Minik is a complex and tragic character, one deserving of a novel. A novel such as this would be as much a portrait of the era in which he lived as a portrait of Minik. So who would be the main characters of this book? They're right there in front of us, hard to improve. There's Minik, of course, but also the vain Peary and Minik's adoptive father, who was fired by the museum for taking kickbacks and who might have spurred Minik in his quest out of his own bitterness toward the museum.

If the real story is hard to improve, why bother with a fictional treatment? There have been several nonfiction books about Minik. Maybe that's enough. Maybe not. Novels can do things and go places that a nonfictional treatment, constrained by fact and reasonable conjecture, must avoid. A novelist can, through her imagination and a substantial amount of research, take on the various roles in the drama. She can effectively become Minik and Peary and Minik's adoptive father, or a reasonable facsimile of any one of them. A novelist can delve beneath the surface into the subconscious of the individual as well as the age, can tell the story between the lines of the nonfictional account. In effect, by reimagining the thoughts and sights of these characters, the novelist gets at a powerful emotional truth that is rarely achieved in any other genre.

Are there any types of newspaper stories that *can't* be transformed into short stories? Not really. All it takes is imagination and curiosity—reading between the lines, discovering the motivations of your characters. If, however, you write the story simply as it appears in the paper, without transforming it, without trying to discover the ambiguities and the mysteries of character and situation, your story will not succeed no matter how interesting the initial idea is. For instance, there's the newspaper story about the beautician who won a $15.7 million Lotto jackpot in September and didn't tell a soul she had the winning ticket. She waited until Christmas, when she gave it to her husband in a card with the inscription, "This is the best I can do this year. I love you." Now that's a great anecdote, a wonderful and touching true-life happening, but will it make a good short story as it stands? Almost certainly not. As life it's fine. But as fiction? Let's say you tell the story from the husband's point of view. His wife has been acting kind of strange lately. He suspects that she's been cheating on him. On Christmas Day she hands him a card. No new drill press like he's been hinting around about for months. Boy, is he disappointed. He opens the card and . . . hey, what's this? A lottery ticket flutters to the floor.

That kind of story simply relies on the surprise ending and as such doesn't show us anything substantial or interesting about these people. If you tell the story from the woman's point of view, it's much the same—maybe even more predictable and sentimental. A good story is neither wholly predictable nor wholly surprising. A good story doesn't rely on simple outcomes. Remember what Sharon Solwitz said about her story, how she ended her story before the protagonist discovers what the results are of her biopsy.

If you write the story about the woman who keeps the lottery ticket a secret till Christmas, think about who she and her husband are, where the conflict is, and ways to transform the actual events—in that order. You might even have to discard the very thing that attracted you to the anecdote in the first place—the woman's self-lessness, her love for her husband. I'm not saying you must do this, but be open to anything that will make the story a good one, that will keep allowing you to make discoveries about your characters and where the story is going. Maybe in your story she winds up *not* giving it to him. Who knows? Or maybe, as in Solwitz's story, the ticket itself will become irrelevant by the end of the story, for good or ill. The central conflict will be something else.

Sketch the plot. Write biographies of the principal characters. Write a possible outcome. Flip the outcome on its head and try it that way. Experiment. Be open-minded. Transform and transform again. Discover the story within the story. Surprise yourself first. Then you can worry about surprising the reader.

DREAMS AND DISCOVERIES

Dreams are part of your life, too. You spend a third of your life asleep, right? So you might as well get something out of it. We often work out problems in our dreams, and even if you're one of those people who claims they don't dream, you should still understand that your subconscious plays a role in your writing. In fact, writing is in some ways a conscious form of dreaming, sitting around in front of a screen or piece of paper and sometimes molding the images, sometimes letting the images form around you out of nothing. Often in a story or a novel you don't know where you're going, much as in a dream, and that sense of mystery is one of the pleasurable things about both writing and dreaming.

Many writers use their dreams as jumping-off points for their stories. David Michael Kaplan's story "Summer People" came from a dream he had, at least the final scene of the story did. "I had a dream in which the prevailing image in the dream was my father swinging out over a lake on a rope swing and falling in, and my feeling of anxiety about this," says Kaplan. "I thought that was interesting so I copied it down in my journal. Later on, that became the final scene in my story."

Several of my own stories have come from dreams, and I make a habit of recording my dreams in my journal when I remember them. One dream I had involved my digging a hole in someone's backyard. I jotted that down, and a couple of years later I was flipping through my notes when I found the mention of the dream and thought it might make a good starting point for a story. The story is called, surprisingly, "Digging a Hole," and it involves a man digging a hole in his ex-wife's backyard. The dramatic question is, of course, why anyone would do such a thing.

Here's how I started the story:

> When Abby, my ex-wife, finally noticed me in her backyard, I was already two feet down. She opened the back door of her house and hurried out.
>
> "Lawrence, what are you doing here!" she said, and positioned herself to my side, so I couldn't swing any more dirt from the hole.

In that opening, I tried not only to set up the dramatic question, but also, by introducing Abby as the man's ex-wife, I give a sense that there's history between the characters, perhaps unresolved conflicts. And, of course, there are — the story is about the internal conflicts of these two characters as reflected in their outward actions.

When I first started this story, I didn't know why the guy was digging the hole, either. I was just as baffled as Abby. I didn't even know who these two people were, and so, as I went along, I had to invent their history. Halfway through the story, I discovered they had lost a child, and this had destroyed their marriage. A similar thing had happened to relatives of mine, but I transformed the circumstances in my story so that, in their particulars, the tragedies were different, only similar in the emotions they brought up. On top of that, I added two characters from my journals, a little girl with a GAF viewmaster and her little brother, riding around nude on a Big Wheel tricycle. I'd encountered this pair back when I was eighteen. When I came to the point where I decided I needed some real live children besides the dead one, I went flipping through my journals and found them. They fit perfectly. I tell you all this simply to show all the different sources of one story. First, I started with a dream, added a family story and even brought my journals into play.

Dreams almost always involve metaphor, simile and symbol. Writing a dream story is almost the opposite of writing other kinds of stories. The dream is already your real life transformed, an inter-

pretation of sorts, so your task is to retransform it into real life—
to make it seem real. Again, you do this through salient detail.
Nobel Prize laureate Gabriel Garcia Marquez says that the more
bizarre a story is, the more detail it should be given so as to make
the world come alive, to make it seem real beyond a doubt. Of
course, not all dreams are bizarre—David Michael Kaplan's dream
about his father, for instance. The dream itself is already quite believable. What needs to be ciphered by the writer is the underlying
emotion of the dream—the anxiety the dreamer feels as he watches
his father fall into the water. Or maybe it's not anxiety. Maybe it's
guilt. Some psychologists would say that Kaplan's dream is actually
a wish-fulfillment dream—a desire to drown the father. Too Freud-
ian? Maybe, but Freud, whatever his faults, understood the underlying contradictions of the human psyche—that whole Faulknerian
idea again of the human heart in conflict with itself. If you understand that people are a mass of contradictions, that they say what
they don't mean and don't mean what they say, you're halfway
home to understanding how to write complex characterizations, to
say nothing of understanding your dreams.

Kaplan understands these contradictions well, as he shows in the
beautiful last scene of his story, which is about a man and his father
returning to a summer home that the father has recently sold. The
mother is dead and the son is newly divorced. The last time the
son visited this summer home he was much younger, and now the
father and son have returned to get everything ready for the new
owners. The relationship is full of tension. The son feels nagged
and belittled by the father, and finally he loses his temper. The
father walks off alone to the lake by the house. It's storming, and
the son anxiously follows him. To the son's surprise, his father grabs
a rope swing tied to a tree limb and walks up a hill:

> His father waved as if in salute, then grasped the thick
> rope with both hands and swung out over the cove, his
> shirt fluttering behind. Frank opened his mouth, but no
> sound came out, the only cry his father's as he reached
> the far point of his arc and let go, the rope falling away
> as he fell, arms swinging, into the lake. He landed bent
> over, partly on his stomach. The water churned where
> he'd entered.

"Dad," Frank murmured in disbelief.

He waited for his father to come up. But he didn't. Nothing moved in the water except the pocking of rain on its surface and the fast receding ripples from his father's plunge.

"Dad?" Frank called. He went onto the dock and peered into the rain-flecked water. The lake was dark: he could see nothing below.

"Dad!" he screamed. "Oh Jesus—" Frank ran to the dock's edge. He tore off one shoe and had the other in his hand when his father surfaced with a whoop farther down the cove. He shook his head like a playful seal and began to breast-stroke slowly toward the dock. Frank sat down, his legs dangling over the edge like a helpless marionette's. He seemed to be laughing and crying at the same time, and try as he might, he couldn't stop. His father must have been confused since he cried out, "What's the matter?" and "What's wrong?" but Frank could only shake his head, and raise his hand, and let it drop.

"I thought you were dead," he said, the words choked, as if it were he that had been drowning. He dropped the other shoe into the water and held out his now empty hands. "I thought you were dead but you weren't."

Notice the ambivalence of emotion in that last line. Notice also how Kaplan has transformed the bare bones of a dream into a believable situation with fully realized characters. He's done this by giving the two characters a sense of history, by letting us see the details of their lives and the conflict between them. Again, it's a matter of distancing yourself from the actual material and reclaiming it or recasting it with the most important tool in your possession, your imagination.

SO-WHAT STORIES

Any of the types of stories mentioned in this chapter can be so-what stories. A so-what story is one based on a job or your childhood in which the only thing that's important about it is that it really happened or it's shocking or it has a punch line. Or it can be a dream story in which the protagonist wakes up at the end, automatically trivializing all the drama of the dream. A so-what story is the story about how much you've always loved Corvettes, and one time you found a great deal on one, but it needed a lot of work, so you spent the whole summer fixing the car—and you did it! It was a beauty when you finished.

Good for you, but so what?

Or you read a newspaper account of some horrific act of violence, a serial rapist/murderer on the loose. You decide to write a story in an attempt to "get into the head" of this character. The results are sadly predictable, an account of a serial rapist/murderer from the point of view of the rapist/murderer. Instead of transforming the story as Joyce Carol Oates did, you simply rely on what we already know, cheap sensationalism, graphic violence and sociopathic reasoning. So what?

Or the time you had a premonition about someone dying, and you told her, but she didn't believe you, and then she really died! Or she didn't!

In either case, so what?

Or a story based solely on feelings of nostalgia. The fact that you feel teary-eyed about the corner malt shop you frequented in the fifties in Riverdale is not necessarily the basis for a great short story or a novel.

Or the time your roommate stole your Corvette, kidnapped your grandmother, and they both died in a fiery crash!

I think you get the point, but if you don't, go back to chapter two. You might want to bone up on the forms of fiction, and the difference between these and anecdotes and memoirs.

A CAVEAT

Of course, all of these categories of writing about yourself are more or less arbitrary forms. A job story can be a childhood story. A family story can be a tell-it-like-it-is story. Or your story might be none of these. The story might be completely fictionalized except for one or two details from your own experience, but that, too, is writing about yourself. In any case, don't take these categories too seriously. They're meant to give you a jump start, not to confine you in any way.

Exercises

1. Use indirection to write a scene based on something traumatic that you witnessed, that happened to you or someone you know. In other words, create some distance by not letting us know everything about your protagonist right away—her motivations, feelings, suspicions. Or take the trauma and transform it to such a degree that it bears little resemblance to the actual event. Remember, the scene should not depend so much on simple outcomes as on character development and understanding.

2. Take the same trauma or a different one and write about it using the head-on approach. Still, you'll need to transform, to cut out unnecessary details and characters.

3. It's true, as Bret Lott says, that the best family stories are often the ones that have been around for ages. Write in your journal any family stories you remember, especially the ones that might get you in trouble. Those are probably the good ones.

4. Write a scene based on a dream. Even if the situation is strange, you'll need to make it believable through salient details and believable characters. Whatever you do, don't tell the reader it's a dream.

5. Pick up today's newspaper and find a story in it that you think could be transformed into a short story. Sketch it out. Who are the main characters? Who is the protagonist? What is the central conflict? Is the conflict something that's been left out of the actual newspaper account? Again, focus on the characters, and transform.

CHAPTER SIX

Real Places

Sometimes a place we've visited fascinates us, and we can't seem to get it out of our system unless we write about it. That's fine as long as the story or novel is more than a thinly disguised travelogue. A story about a family trip in high school to Hawaii is probably not going to mesmerize an audience.

Every once in a while an Arctic tundra story crosses my path. These are usually tales of high adventure in which two characters, usually men, fly around in a plane somewhere in Alaska, when the plane suddenly loses power and down they go. The rest of the story deals with their attempts at survival. We are informed that the Arctic tundra is freezing and that it's very white. Does that convince you that you're experiencing the Arctic tundra along with these men? It doesn't do it for me. It's your job as the writer to convince us that we're in the world you've created, not the reader's job to believe, and you convince the reader through the sensory details you choose to convey a place. Inevitably, such stories focus solely on unbelievable plot developments, and the characters tend to be about as believable as the descriptions of the frozen waste. But place or setting in a work of fiction can be a vital element. Often, the setting functions as almost a distinct character in the work, with its own personality — weaknesses, hopes, dreams and fears. If you write convincingly about a place, this might be the secret ingredient to make your story or novel come alive. In this chapter, we'll discuss strategies for writing convincingly about real places.

PLACES IN MEMORY

The places we remember are often the richest sources for our fictional settings. Just as childhood memories can serve as the springboard for our stories, so too can our childhood homes and neighborhoods inform and inspire these stories. Before beginning to write such a story, ask yourself a few questions. What do you remember most from your childhood home? List the furnishings. Take a mental tour, first starting at the front door and going through all the rooms. Take your time. Lift your grandmother's teapot off the mantle—you know, the teapot that played "Tea for Two" when you lifted it. Notice the aromas. What's your grandmother cooking? Take a peek outside. If it's a fair day, take a walk. Go through the neighborhood. Wave to your friends and acquaintances. It's been a long time. "What's that you're carrying?" they might ask.

"Oh, it's my journal," you tell them, scribbling a few notes as you chat.

"Oh . . . well, say hi to your grandma for me," they say.

"Sure thing."

If you do this exercise, a flood of memories is bound to come back to you. You'll be surprised by how much you remember. Write down every detail of this place. When you write your story or novel, many of these details will come in handy and help transport your reader to this place in the same way you were transported.

Of course, you won't recall everything. Some things you'll remember incorrectly. Sometimes you'll remember too much. As with any kind of fiction, you must learn to choose. Use only those details of your setting that are necessary to convey the place to the reader.

Nanci Kincaid's first novel was a semi-autobiographical coming-of-age story called *Crossing Blood* (Putnam). It's about a young white girl who lives in segregated Tallahassee during the sixties, in the last house on California Street before the black neighborhood begins. When Kincaid wrote the novel, she was living in Wyoming and could not get back to Tallahassee to do research. She'd lived there for eight years when she was a child and had moved away when she was thirteen. She had to rely solely on her memory for the details.

"I saw the place the way memory glorifies things a little bit,"

Kincaid says. "There were many things that I'd forgotten and didn't remember, but the things I remembered I was very unsure of because I hadn't lived there since I was a child. So I embellished a few things. I couldn't remember the name of a certain restaurant so I made one up. I started blending the true facts with artificial details. I put a trailer park in the book that wasn't really there. What it had really been was old barracks that my parents had once lived in, army barracks that had been converted to student use. But you know how barracks look kind of long and industrial. I'd remembered them as trailers. I write about a place called the Bluebird that was in Frenchtown. There was really such a place but I don't think the name of it was the Bluebird. I never could remember the name.

"The thing that I most wanted to capture about the place was the heat. The heat in Tallahassee is above and beyond anything I've ever experienced anywhere else. Because of that heat people wore very few clothes, especially boys. I remember boys never wore shirts. Nobody wore shoes. It was kind of a shorts culture. I wanted the junglelike quality of it all to come across. There were lots of vines and palmetto leaves. When we were little and watched Tarzan movies, which were supposed to be the African jungle, it always looked like Tallahassee, like our backyard.

"Also, because I was writing about blacks and whites, I wanted to capture the sense of how in *my* mind Tallahassee had a lot of the terrain that I supposed you would find if you went to Africa: the heat and the jungle and the vegetation and the snakes climbing everywhere. Wildlife was very real. In the early chapters of the book, I had things like finding possums. We used to find possums in our trash can every morning. We'd take them up the road and give them to a neighbor who ate them. But then, only a mile or so from us was this pristine white capitol building. But it seemed like far, far away."

Kincaid didn't need to write these details down in a journal to evoke them in her novel. You can see how firmly planted the Tallahassee of the sixties is from the above description. She obviously knows this place inside out, even if she misses a few details here and there. That's not important. Absolute accuracy is not the point in a fictional landscape. You want the feel of the place to seem real—though if you're writing about a real place like Tallahassee, you have two audiences: the people who live in Tallahassee and know the place better than you, and the people who may never have set foot in Tallahassee in their lives. You have different obligations to these audiences and they, in turn, have different expectations. Often, the former audience cares deeply whether you got the details right, and if you didn't you can expect a letter from a local who will upbraid you for your lack of verisimilitude, even if that only amounts to putting a trailer park where, in fact, an old army barracks used to be. The latter audience, those who've never set foot in Tallahassee, care how well you're able to transport them to a place they've never been and make them feel the jungle heat, the insects, the wildlife. Neither audience should be discounted.

The distance that memory provides when writing about a place can benefit your fiction. When you are emotionally, temporally and geographically distant from a place, you are often more able to see it with the clarity of a frieze. You will not remember everything, but you will remember what's important to you. Kincaid is correct when she points out that memory tends to glorify a place, but for the purposes of fiction, that's good. In our fiction, we want to glorify our settings, make them larger than life, give them the mythic proportions of the African jungle or the Himalayan mountains. What you remember about a place is the feeling it gave you, and the details are imbued with that feeling. Writers are essentially myth-makers, and the myths they keep returning to are primarily concerned with origins. Where we grew up is the site of our own personal myth of creation, and when we write about the place of our childhood, we are concerned with creation, the formation of our own perceptions against the backdrop of this mythical world, whether Edenlike or after the Fall.

PLACES CLOSE TO HOME

You can also write about a place you live in now, though it might be so familiar that you're unaware how rich a source it can be for your fiction. What you need is distance, the kind you naturally achieve in your memories. Sometimes it's difficult to see this place in perspective. So you need to step back, either physically or mentally. You could take a vacation and write notes in your journal while you're away. But that's not realistic for most of us. It's not often we take vacations, and when we do, the last thing we want to do is write about the place we just left. The best way to achieve distance is to do it mentally, by transforming either your point of view or your immediate surroundings. If you live in an old house, imagine who the original occupants were, and write a story from their point of view. E.L. Doctorow did this and came up with his famous novel *Ragtime*, a book set at the turn of the century whose primary setting is the house he was living in. Or take a walk around your block. Who's that elderly man who peeks out at you whenever you leave your house? Maybe you could write a story from his point of view. Eudora Welty was looking out her window one day when she saw an elderly woman crossing her field. She wondered where the woman was headed, and from that random sighting came her story "A Worn Path" about an elderly woman's journey into town for the sake of love. You might take a different path. Take a walk to the doughnut shop on the corner of your street with its red neon sign flashing. Go in and take notes. Order a few doughnuts and some coffee so you won't look suspicious. Look at the people in the back making doughnuts. Write a story from one of their points of view. You might need to interview someone who works there for accuracy, or you can rely on your imagination. In any case, there are stories all around you. Keep your eyes open.

THE ROLE OF PLACE

Above all, remember that this is a story or novel you're writing. Character, again, is what needs to be stressed, and while the place might become a kind of character in your narrative, don't allow it to overwhelm your characters and story. You might write an accurate and beautiful description of the town of Charlotte Amalie on the island of St. Thomas, but if you go on for page after page, you most likely will bore the reader. In fact, any description of a place should probably be anchored within a character's consciousness, and say as much about the character as it does about the place.

Take a look at the opening paragraph from Robert Onopa's "The Man Who Swam Through Jellyfish, Through Men-of-War":

> Kimo Akeo owned a cream-colored Cessna from which
> he spotted fish for his sons. In the clear Hawaiian air, he

flew in an elegant, extended zigzag pattern over waters he had set nets in when he was young: those of the Kaiwi Channel from the westerly shore of Molokai to the easterly shore of Oahu; from Makapuu Point in the north, south to the Penguin Banks. In the moving waters of the channel — seas blue-green and brilliant whose vast bulk was furrowed by the wind and heaved by swells — his fifty-year-old eyes could distinguish schools of nehu, anchovies, swimming in shimmering circles just beneath the surface, or aku bonita, whose fins breaking water turned it foamy white in circles a hundred yards wide.

Note that this description shows a lot about the character of Kimo Akeo. What is it that this character focuses on, to the exclusion of almost all else? Fish. There isn't a description in this paragraph that doesn't end with a mention of fish. If Onopa had chosen to describe at length the clouds in the sky above the Cessna, he might have lost his focus and diluted our understanding of Akeo's character.

Here's a question that might seem out of left field, but it's pertinent to our discussion: Does cultural identity or ethnicity have any bearing on your ability to write authoritatively about a place? Could and should a non-Yanamamo Indian write about the Amazon from a Yanamamo point of view? How about a non-Haitian writing about Port-au-Prince or the Haitian enclave in Miami? If your answer is no, you're discounting the role of the imagination in literature, and what you really want to read and/or write is nonfiction. If you demand that the writer of a fictional work be, in the narrow sense, what he is writing of, you have very little understanding of what fiction is. Of course, we make assumptions, rightly or wrongly, about a writer based on his or her name. If the writer's first name is Elizabeth and she's writing from a man's point of view, we pay closer attention to how accurate the point of view seems. If the writer's last name is Dominguez and she's writing about the town of Merida on the Yucatan Peninsula, we think, "Ah, Dominguez. She must really know the Yucatan with a name like that!"

But that's a silly criterion to go by. Just because you were born in Charleston, South Carolina, or grew up there, or buried two sets of great-grandparents there, does not mean you can write worth a lick about the place. In fact, as shocking as this might seem, a native New Yorker might be able to write about Charleston better than you.

Take Robert Onopa, for instance. What assumptions did you make about him when you read his name and then read the passage from his story? Let's see. Onopa? Is that a Hawaiian name? Could be. Sounds kind of Japanese to me. Well, you know there's a large population of Japanese-Americans in Hawaii. The fact is, Robert Onopa, who teaches in the English Department at the University of Hawaii, is a *haole* (if you don't know what *haole* is you'll just have to go to Hawaii to find out), and his last name is Polish. Does that change your opinion of the passage of his story I quoted?

It shouldn't.

As I've said, people often feel a sense of ownership of their experiences. They feel the same about the place they grew up, especially if it has some history like Charleston or a cultural uniqueness like Hawaii. When someone's ethnic identity is closely tied to a place, she might feel violated or exploited by your making fictional forays into her territory—no matter how convincing the portrait might be. Sometimes people feel that their territory is being co-opted when an outsider writes about them from their point of view. One well-known writer, serving as a judge on an arts panel, not only refused to award money to an artist who she learned was not of the same race as her fictional characters, but went so far as to call the surprised writer on the phone and castigate her for having such temerity. And a major magazine recently rejected a story that they had previously accepted after belatedly learning that the race of the writer and his characters did not match.

As Margot Livesey insightfully remarks in her essay "How to Tell a True Story," "In the current climate, a novel set in Vietnam, written by someone who had not been there, would be unlikely to meet with the rapturous reception of *The Red Badge of Courage*. Certain experiences—war, other races, some illnesses, perhaps other sexual orientations—are no longer deemed appropriate territory for the imagination. We want the writer to be writing out of memory." But, of course, this expectation is ridiculous. Neither experience nor imagination should be privileged over the other. A fiction writer is not a nonfiction writer. If we ask our fiction writers to simply write about what they "know" in the narrowest, most corporeal sense of that word, we should also require actors to stop acting and painters to stop painting—unless they paint strict representations of their lives. Charles Johnson, author of *Middle Passage* (Atheneum), a novel about a slave ship that won the National Book Award in 1990, concurs. In an interview in the *AWP Chronicle*, he says, "Writers have always been able to transpose themselves into not just the racial other, but the sexual other and also into other historical periods. . . . Writers have always done that and always will do that regardless of people who, for one political reason or another, feel that their territory is being appropriated. . . . That other argument means knowledge is racially bound. That's scary. Ultimately, that is racist."

To which I might add: You cannot co-opt the territory of the imagination because it is a limitless territory without boundaries, without rulers. The story you write will always be different, without exception, from the story I write, regardless of whether our source material is the same.

Let's take this a step further. Can you write about a place you've never been? Nobel Prize winner Saul Bellow wrote his novel *Henderson the Rain King* (Viking Penguin), a book about an eccentric American millionaire's adventures in Africa, without ever having set foot on the continent. Robert Louis Stevenson wrote *Treasure Island* before visiting the South Pacific (where he later went to live). And what about novels that take place in a different time period? T. Correghesan Boyle's novel, *Water Music* (Viking Penguin), about a Scottish explorer, is set several hundred years ago in Africa. Obviously, an act of the imagination is necessary to transport oneself and one's readers back into time. Robert Fox, a writer from Ohio, wrote a story, "Her Story-His Story," that won a prestigious Nelson Algren Award, from the point of view of a black inmate in prison. Fox, who works for the Ohio Arts Council, *has* seen prison, but only as an outsider, as a teacher and workshop leader. He tells of how a group of inmates read his story and were shocked when they met him and saw he was white. Their reaction, however, was overwhelmingly positive. What shocked these inmates more than Fox's race was how well he described the prison. In his story, Fox describes the prison as it was twenty years ago and how it's changed since then. For that portion of the story, he relied completely on his imagination. He hadn't seen the prison twenty years ago. One prisoner could hardly believe that. He was something of a prison historian and claimed that Fox had the details exactly right.

This approach is not universally successful by any means. There's nothing worse than a clumsy story that relies on stereotypes about a place one has never been and a point of view one has never known. But the imagination is a powerful thing. "I've written about places without having been there," says Barry Hannah. "And when I got there, I had guessed pretty well. I think that the foreigner or the alien often has a point of view that is more precise than the native. I used to not believe that but I do now. It's good that a New Yorker would cover the South and that a Southerner would cover New York."

I'm not saying it's good to be ignorant of the place you write about. That's absurd. The contrary is true. It's important to find out as much as possible about a place before you write about it, and it's important to strive for authenticity, something we'll discuss in the next chapter. All I'm saying here is that it's possible.

It's all in the details. If you rely on the obvious and the stereotypical when writing from a point of view that's not your own, about a place that's not your own, you will not be successful. Even those who know a place intimately sometimes rely on the stereotypical in writing about that place. Think of it as a test of your imagination. If you set a story in New York, don't have your character stand in front of Trump Towers, arms over his head, yelling, "You crazy, wacky city! I love you!" If you write about New York, better to include lesser-known landmarks, a particular Korean grocery on Broadway or a dry cleaner. The more particular and individual the details, the more believable they seem.

ADOPTING A PLACE

As I've stated, many writers adopt a locale to write about in their fiction. It might be a place they live in now but weren't born in, a place they've passed through, or one they've never been. Success depends on the imagination and skill of the writer, not on his physical ties to the place.

Sometimes a place you've never lived in captures your imagination, as it did with Philip Gerard when he wrote *Hatteras Light* (Scribner), a novel set in the early part of this century about a life-saving crew on the Outer Banks of North Carolina. Now Gerard lives in North Carolina, in Wilmington, another coastal town, but when he wrote about Hatteras he was living in Arizona. He'd spent a lot of time in Hatteras and says, "The land had kind of whipped into my bones. I kept on dreaming of it and thinking about it." Gerard's latest book, *Cape Fear Rising* (John F. Blair), is set in Wilmington in 1898. He says the same thing happened to him with Wilmington as Hatteras: "As I began walking around the streets the ghosts started coming out of the cracks in the sidewalk and the river. There's this tremendous feeling of place. There's this weight of history. And the closer you get to the heart of downtown Wilmington the thicker the air gets with those spirits. And in certain buildings it's practically overpowering." To write successfully about a place, you must be overpowered by it. If it doesn't "whip into your bones," your treatment will most likely be superficial or naive or overly romanticized.

Bret Lott's novel, *Reed's Beach* (Pocket Books), takes place in a day and deals with a man and a woman who have lost a child and have retreated to an isolated beach on the New Jersey shore to start healing themselves. Lott stumbled upon this beach in 1982 and decided he would someday write about it. He was in graduate school in Massachusetts at the time, and he and his wife often traveled to New Jersey to visit her parents. One day, the four of them were driving along the Delaware-side Jersey shore, when they saw a sign for Reed's Beach. "We wondered what the heck was Reed's Beach," Lott says. "Melanie's father was driving, and he was game for anything. We just turned down the dirt road and followed it out and across this big marsh plain, and out there at the end was this strip of run-down shabby cottages. There was barely anybody out there. We just went from one end of the place to the other, and there was something very strange about being there. As a writer you're always training yourself to look at everything, to take everything in. I was struck by this place, how remote it was, how quiet it was. It seemed to have this tone all its own, and I wanted to catch it somehow. It was a visual thing, but it was the *feel* of that visual that stayed with me.

"I decided years before I started writing it that I was going to write the book based on this place sometime. After I wrote *Jewel*, I decided that now was the time to write about this place, so I went up there in February and stayed there for three or four days and just drove the streets of the town, Cape May, up and down, up and down. I picked up little flyers everywhere of things to do, places to see. I took a notebook. As I went around, I'd stop and write down the names of the streets. I'd write down names of stores. I picked up the local newspaper and circled things that I thought were interesting, and went to the local library. I'd decided I wanted to set the book in February, this little place at its most remote time. So I looked at the community bulletin board to see what kind of events were taking place in this resort town in February. And I used all that. I had someone walk into the library and look at the community bulletin board and see that there really wasn't much going on.

"And I took photographs. When I returned, I set all these photos on my desk when I was writing—and I kept looking at them. Mainly, there was a particular house that was actually on Reed's Beach that I wrote about. It just seemed to be the right house, although in the book it's a little different. When I had pictures of this house perched right there on my computer, it gave me that tone, that texture that I wanted."

Lott says the actual landscape didn't undergo any major transformations in the book. Some houses had different locations and he moved the grocery store, but for the most part things stayed right where they are in real life. He says he doesn't like to invent landscapes. The real landscape gives him an anchor that he doesn't have to worry about, so he's able to devote his creative energies to what he says is the hard thing: inventing the people and discovering their motivations, their vulnerabilities and strengths. "In the midst of trying to make all that stuff believable, I don't also want to have to worry about inventing the landscape," he says. "I really believe in using what's there because the hard work is making the characters come to life."

Even though Lott came up with the landscape first, notice how his emphasis is on the characters. Once he had the landscape, he still had to decide what the story was going to be and whose story it was. Obviously, the type of landscape and the melancholy and desolate feelings it gave him suggested the type of story he might write with this landscape as a backdrop. He had previously written a short short story called "Night," about a man who makes a nightly pilgrimage to his deceased son's room, thinking he can hear his child breathing. But Lott felt that he needed a much larger canvas to paint the story of a parent's grief for a dead child—and he felt that Reed's Beach was the place to tell this larger story.

DISGUISING A PLACE

Just as one can write a composite character, one can write a composite place. Often, the disguise is a thin one, meant to fool no one. All the same, calling your great eastern city "Metropolis" instead of "New York" gives you all sorts of freedom. First, you're signaling the reader, the persnickety one I mentioned earlier, the one who won't go beyond the accuracy of the details when reading your book. You're telling everyone, including yourself, that this is a book of fiction and the place you're writing about is as mythical as the home of the gods, Mt. Olympus—which, of course, is also the name of a real mountain in Greece. And by a strange twist, you're actually appeasing this reader by using this strategy. You're turning the tables on her. Instead of saying, "Ferret out all the inaccuracies in my book," you're appealing to this reader as a fellow insider who's not fooled one bit by your thin disguise. You're telling her, "Guess what's really true in my story." And before you know it, that reader will think she has it all figured out. "Why, that's Mr. Simpkin's house," she'll exclaim, even if you have no idea who Mr. Simpkin is, much less where he lives.

But there are other reasons to disguise a place in your fiction. Perhaps you don't want to hurt the feelings of your friends and family who live in your hometown, who you believe will be devastated by an unflattering portrait of the place. Or maybe you once witnessed a knife fight in a bar in Chicago and you've decided to include a scene based on that memory in your novel. Chances are slim, of course, that the owners of that bar will read your book, but you never know. If you've written an unflattering portrait of the place, the owner might become angry enough to sue you. I'll talk more about that in chapter eight, but the point is, don't leave yourself vulnerable to legal action. If you're in doubt, change the locale. Base it on the real bar, but place it in another city. Change the name. Invent another city. Maybe the knife fight doesn't need to take place in a bar at all. Transfer the knife fight to an upscale restaurant and see how that changes the story. Turn the knives into water pistols, pads of butter, croquet mallets. As with anything in fiction, be willing to be flexible with real events and open to the transformation process.

Nanci Kincaid's new novel, *Balls*, about the wife of a football coach, takes place in a town that's based on Birmingham, Alabama. "Place is more symbolic in the book I'm writing now," she says. "It was more specific in the first book. I'm writing about a fictional university. It's not going to be Auburn or the University of Alabama. It's going to be Birmingham University." Doing this frees her from the facts, allows her to transform the world to her specifications. "I don't want to be held to the factual parts: who the coaches were that year, what the offense was, what the record was. Those kinds of facts I'm not too interested in. That's the kind of book for a sportswriter to write. I just want to capture the flavor of a football-obsessed culture, how it marries the spiritual culture and becomes the religion. Even if place names are fictional, since I'm making the book *conspicuously* camouflaged, I think a lot of readers there will know that the story is true even if the place names aren't."

That's an important point. Sticking to the bare facts does not necessarily make a story true or a place seem real. What's important is the feeling or tone of the place, as Bret Lott refers to it. And even though Bret Lott and Nanci Kincaid have different approaches to place, she is, in her own words, more "forgiving of herself" for not having every detail an exact mirror of the way it is in reality. Still, the details she uses capture the place, *could* be true of the place. Does it matter if the street you lived on had barracks or trailers? If the feeling you get from the word "barracks" is virtually the same feeling you get from the word "trailers," it doesn't matter. Both connote a kind of temporariness and a lack of financial means. For the purposes of your story, trailers might work a lot better.

As Kincaid states, she uses the landscape of Birmingham symbolically. "I've made up names of apartment complexes that may or may not turn out to be real places. Birmingham's favorite symbol is the Vulcan, a big iron statue which sits on the highest point in Birmingham. All around there are things called Vulcan Drive, Vulcan Apartments. So I just made up The Vulcan Arms Apartment Building. I borrow symbolic things that I know about the city, but it's very nonspecific."

Some details are more important to her than others — mostly

those that give the reader the flavor of the place. So while she may not be concerned with actual place names or actual football coaches or whether the Birmingham Shoneys was next to the Esso station, she plans on getting a Birmingham phone directory. Not only the names will be useful to give her that flavor (of course, she won't use anyone's real full name), but the Yellow Pages too, even the size and weight of the phone book to give her a sense of the size and weight of the city.

Sometimes she calls up her ex-husband, who is in real life a football coach, to ask him about Birmingham because he knows the city better than her. "I needed to know the name of a high school that was a football powerhouse twenty years ago. I didn't want to make that up. Then he told me what it was and I was crushed. I was so disappointed. The Shades Valley Mounties. And I just hated it. What in the world was Birmingham doing with a team called the Mounties? It turned out that I kind of got attached to it."

The more you know about a place, the more tools (in the form of details) you have to convey that place to the reader. But it's your choices that count, not the exactness of your terrain. All the details in the world won't make a place come alive if you haven't anchored those details in the mind of a believable, sympathetic and vital character. And the fact that you're accurate doesn't necessarily mean your details will seem believable. As I've said before, just because something is true doesn't make it believable. The Shades Valley Mounties is a case in point. Never in a million years could you make up a detail like that. If you didn't know anything about Birmingham, Alabama, and wanted to name a fictitious football team, what would you come up with? The most obvious name would have something to do with the Confederacy: the Rebels, perhaps. Or an animal name: maybe the Cougars. But the Mounties? It's so unlikely, so unexpected that it *is* believable. These kinds of details are exactly why we borrow from real life in our fiction. They enrich and enliven our fiction. Sometimes real life just can't be improved upon.

Exercises

1. Write a scene with a character based on someone you know well in an unfamiliar setting (unfamiliar to this character but familiar to you) — Aunt Betty from Tulsa riding the Chicago El or Uncle Lou from New York showing up unannounced at your apartment. Write this scene from this character's point of view. Now switch. Tell the story from your point of view. How does your description of the setting change from one point of view to the other? Are some details missing in the version based on your point of view? Why?

2. Take a mental tour of the neighborhood in which you grew up. Pay attention to all the details. Get reacquainted with the place. Are there any stories lurking in the streets, the houses, the fields of your past?

3. Take a mental tour of your present neighborhood. Where are the stories here? Pay attention to every sight and sound, and sniff out the stories.

4. Write a scene from the point of view of the person who lived in your house or apartment originally (as E.L. Doctorow did in *Ragtime*), or the person who lived there right before you, or even the person you imagine will move in after you. Have you left anything behind, forgotten anything — clothes, furniture, money — that the next resident will wonder about?

5. Disguise a place you know well. Write a scene about this place, changing whatever aspects of the locale will make you feel free to explore the terrain with your imagination. Think of the place symbolically. What symbols will best convey the feeling or tone of this disguised locale?

CHAPTER SEVEN

Writing (and Rewriting) With Authority

Throughout the creative process, you must try to mold your story to the specifications of fiction. As in the other stages of writing, your revisions involve a constant search for structure, flexibility, distance and the right point of view. Everything you write won't be immediately brilliant. In fact, very little will be. The real art of writing is in the fashioning, the revision of the story. If you don't give up, if you're persistent, you can turn almost anything into a good story. In this chapter we'll discuss the strategies for making your story as good as possible, from research to revision.

RESEARCH

Obviously, you don't have to write from your own experience. The standard advice used to be to "write what you know," but what does that mean? What you know is not a static thing. We're all capable of learning more. And that's where research comes in. If you don't know something, find out about it. A lot of fiction writers use research in their work—everyone from James Michener, who has a researcher working for him on his mammoth epics, to lesser-known writers working on tiny short stories.

Research for a fiction writer can involve just about anything. When we think of research, we think of someone cloistered among the stacks of a library, poring through dusty texts. But that's only one kind of research. There are two categories of research: *primary* and *secondary*. Primary research involves traveling to a place you're writing about, actually running with the bulls in Pamplona or interviewing one of the Watergate conspirators. Secondary research involves reading a book about the place you're writing about, watching a film of the running of the bulls or listening to an interview with Gordon Liddy. Both types are equally valid for the fiction writer, as long as the final product seems authentic to the reader.

Remember what we talked about in the last chapter? Even if you've lived somewhere does not mean you have the ability to write convincingly about the place. The opposite is true as well. Even if you haven't been somewhere doesn't mean you're unable to write convincingly about the place. As I mentioned, if that were the case, historical novels would be impossible, to say nothing of science fiction. Travel isn't necessary to write convincingly about a place, provided you do your research and are able to use it authoritatively in a fictional context. But those are major provisos.

If you want to write a novel set in Borneo, find out as much about Borneo as possible. Read about the culture, the flora and fauna, the climate. You can learn a lot about a place from a book or photographs. Watch a documentary on Borneo. Learn from the experience of others; interview people who've spent time there. Look at the microfilm of the *Borneo Times* or another paper in the library. If your story takes place in 1955, find out about the time. But don't just look at the articles. Look at the ads, what people were wearing in Borneo, what was playing at the movie theater.

Knowing When to Stop

The problem with research is that you never know when to stop. Naturally, you want things to be accurate, and most good writers are perfectionists, so you keep on reading about Borneo until you've read twenty-five books on the subject, have amassed a video library, and can speak every dialect on the island. But you still haven't started your novel. If you're not careful, you never will — and your research will become a kind of crutch.

It doesn't matter how you organize your research. Index cards, your journal, a tape recorder, a photo album. What's important is for you not to let the research get out of hand. This might sound a little strange, but in your first draft rely on nothing but your imagination, especially if you find yourself bogged down in interminable research. Your imagination, if it's working properly, is a pretty amazing tool, and sometimes fact and imagination coincide.

Then, after you have a workable draft on paper, go back and fill the gaps with research. This method works perfectly well. You just have to slog through and be unabashed in your ignorance during the writing of the first draft. You can change it later.

In rare instances, if your imagination is powerful enough and the world you've created is believable, it doesn't necessarily have to be authentic. A number of years ago, I read a review in *The New York Times Book Review* of a novel written by a French woman. The novel was set in Greenwich Village, where the novelist had never set foot and didn't know much about. Nevertheless, the reviewer, though somewhat bemused, gave the book a favorable review, saying that this was a strange hybrid of Greenwich Village and a neighborhood in Paris, but it didn't matter because the book was engaging and believable within the context it had created.

And the French artist Henri Rousseau was a postal clerk in Paris whose paintings all depicted scenes from Africa, where he had never set foot. The giant plants in his jungle scenes were merely large-scale versions of plants that could be found in France. Rousseau's paintings have a fairy-tale quality, but the scenes they depict seem authentic in their own way, just as a good fairy tale will draw the reader in and say something authentic about the human condition.

Incorporating Research

When I wrote *The Last Studebaker*, I found all kinds of books about Studebakers and lined my shelves with them. I also had a videotape of a documentary done on Studebakers and pamphlets on various homes the Studebaker family had owned in South Bend, Indiana, where the Studebaker plant was located and the novel is set. I put a map of South Bend on my wall, bought a weather calendar, drank coffee out of a Studebaker mug, had a Studebaker refrigerator magnet and a Studebaker T-shirt.

I read these books, pondered my map, rewound the videotape and diligently drank coffee from my Studebaker mug. After a while, I knew a good deal about Studebakers. The problem was that I wasn't writing a history of the Studebaker car or family; I was writing a novel. And while Studebakers are an integral part of the novel, they function primarily on the level of metaphor. The heart of the novel is about a family who lives in present-day South Bend, twenty-five years after the shutdown of the Studebaker plant. The main character's father used to work at the plant and suffered a breakdown when it closed, but there are other concerns in her life besides the ancient legacy of Studebaker.

Still, there was plenty of lore I wanted to include in the book. For instance, in the annual Christmas parade through downtown South Bend the year before the plant closed, the organizers flocked a Studebaker. I loved this image of a flocked car, but unfortunately, I just couldn't fit it in. There were also wonderful facts about the company, some of which I was able to incorporate, some of which I couldn't. One early draft had a restaurant scene between my main character, Lois, and her ex-husband, Willy, in which Willy rather baldly spouts facts about Studebaker to his bored ex-wife and bored reader. I knew it was bad the moment I wrote it, but I guess I just needed to get it out.

This is what's commonly referred to as *exposition disguised as dialogue*. It's not necessarily bad to incorporate your research into your dialogue, but your dialogue should never seem as though it was written for the sole purpose of conveying information. Likewise, you don't need to incorporate all of your research in one large, undigestible chunk. Weave it through your story. Exposition slows down a story, so use it sparingly so that you don't bog down the reader. Also ask yourself why you want to incorporate this or that fact in your novel or story. Is it simply because it's an interesting tidbit? Or does it enrich the story? In a novel, you have more leeway than in a short story. You can be a little more self-indulgent, throwing in a few tidbits—whether about Studebakers or Borneo—simply because you like them. I placed many of my tidbits in the mouth of an auctioneer as he auctions a classic Studebaker toward the end of the novel.

A related problem is that you must find the right way to convey the information gathered in your research. Sometimes a story becomes more like an essay when you try to incorporate the facts you've found. Are all of the facts you've found absolutely necessary to your story? Is it essential that we know the per capita income of Borneo residents? Many details in a story or a novel are not absolutely crucial for the reader to know. And even if they are crucial, you must find a way to trick the reader into not noticing he is learning about a different time or place.

WRITING WITH AUTHORITY

What the French novelist writing about Greenwich Village suc-
ceeded in doing is commonly known as *writing with authority*. Terms
like this and *writing honestly* are often bandied about in workshops
without anyone really knowing how to achieve either state, except
instinctively. As for writing honestly, that's a potentially dangerous
term (though I've used it myself) that could lead writers to gush
all over the page or write something autobiographical without
transforming it at all. Writing with authority is an equally mysterious term. You can get all the research right. You can know your
subject. But when you start writing, it doesn't seem convincing,
for any number of reasons, perhaps as numerous and individual
as the number of writers who have written stories that didn't ring
true. But one overwhelming reason has to do with what David
Huddle in *The Writing Habit: Essays* (Gibbs Smith) calls writing with
the "false self." He explains that most often "the false self is an
overly literary fellow, a user of fancy diction and elaborate syntax,
a manipulator of characters who are too good and beautiful for this
world or else . . . thoroughly terrible and evil." The writer of such
a story is perhaps more concerned with being literary or appearing
smart to be bothered with an understanding of her characters. Often, such a writer is trying to imitate another writer she admires.
This is fine; learning through imitation is a perfectly respectable
avenue — as long as you eventually cast off the imitative voice and
find the voice that's most natural for you.

Ian MacMillan is one writer who writes authoritatively about a
time and place he did not experience. He grew up in upstate New
York and has taught for many years at the University of Hawaii.
Sometimes he writes what he calls "cows and chainsaw stories"
about New York, but most often his subject is Eastern Europe
during World War II. His novel *Orbit of Darkness* (Harcourt Brace
Jovanovich) is an amazing exploration of the human spirit pushed
to extremes, and it unblinkingly explores the war from disparate
points of view. One constant character in the book is the historical
figure Maximillian Kolbe, a Franciscan priest who volunteered to
take another man's place in a starvation cell at Auschwitz. Another
story in the novel is from the point of view of a Ukrainian separatist
fighting the Germans, and one of the most powerful chapters of

the book is from the point of view of a young German prisoner in a Russian P.O.W. camp. MacMillan is not for everyone. His vision is often harrowing. But it is so precise and, at its core, humane, that his work never treads on the sensational. The chapter from the point of view of the German P.O.W. is called "The Smallest Circle." Here's how it begins:

> Southeast of Moscow, February, 1943
>
> Klaus Fenske bends over one end of the crosscut saw, dizzy and stupid with fatigue and hunger. The man he thinks of as the Fatalist is on the other end, working the smooth wooden handle with his stubbed off fingers, breath vapor curling away from his bowed head. Fenske's eyes are locked with a demented attention on the Fatalist's hands moving away, then close, then away, in a dreamlike, mesmerizing rhythm. The butts of the Fatalist's half-length fingers are still scabbed over, but healing. His left hand still has a ring finger and a little finger, which look to Fenske like the toes of a diseased bird clutching the handle. He has let his two remaining fingernails and his thumbnails grow more than a centimeter long.

This passage is written with authority. Remember that the best way to incorporate your research is to anchor your "facts" in the consciousness of your main character, as MacMillan does with his character Fenske. The details are specific, and the voice is simple but commanding, and the action is immediate. The idea for this story sprang from a tiny mention in one of the books MacMillan was researching for his novel. He read that one method of execution in Russia during the war was to hammer a bullet into the base of a prisoner's skull, thereby severing his spinal cord. Admittedly, pretty gruesome stuff, but the story that sprang from this tiny mention is strangely beautiful.

THE REVISION PROCESS

One aspect of writing with authority is the revision process. In fact, the revision process, for most writers, is perhaps the single most important ingredient in writing believable fiction. It's here that the real art happens, that the necessary adjustments and overhauls are made to your story. A bad ending, for example, can ruin an otherwise good story. Often, in revising, you find the right ending for your story, and afterward you can't imagine it ever having ended differently. Or perhaps you need more details. Or maybe you've included an unnecessary character in your story, one who played an important role in the real event but who now seems to serve no real purpose. And of course, nearly every time you add something to a piece of fiction, something else has to be taken away to maintain the story's balance. And nearly every time you take something away, something new needs to be added.

When I was twelve, I bought props for practical jokes out of catalogs. Fake vomit, fake dog doo, snapping packs of gum, cigarette loads, itching powder. You name it. But the best thing I got that year was something called the Big Ear. This was a listening device, a giant orange cone with a tripod and a little ear plug to listen with. With the Big Ear, I could listen to conversations almost five hundred yards away. My mom and I lived in Columbia, Missouri, at the time, where she taught at Stephens College, and I used to take the Big Ear out to Stephens Lake and point it at couples making out. Sometimes they'd look up at me and wonder, *What's that kid doing?* Then I'd tip the cone up toward the sun and pretend I was conducting some serious scientific experiment.

Stephens was an all-girls school, and I had crushes on my mom's students. My favorite was a woman named Nan. Nan smoked a lot and I was against smoking, so one time when Nan came over, I placed a cigarette load in one of her smokes, thinking she might get the message that smoking was bad if the cigarette blew up in her face. I also thought it would be funny. It was hilarious. I caught her dress on fire, but luckily Nan wasn't hurt, and she still miraculously liked me.

One time, my mom left me for a few days with one of her students, a woman named Robin. My mom was going to Denver for an ear operation. An old boyfriend of Robin's found out where she was staying and kidnapped both her and me. He drove us around for a while, babbling and getting angrier and angrier. I didn't know what was going on. He stopped on a dirt road and told me to walk up the road out of sight. I didn't hear anything for about fifteen minutes. Finally, Robin came and got me. "It's all right," she said. "He's going to take us home." And that was the end of it. After the man dropped us off, Robin didn't call the police and she made me promise I wouldn't tell my mother what had happened. I promised because I really didn't know what *had* happened. I forgot the entire experience until I started writing a story about the Big Ear some twenty years later.

I thought this incident and the one involving Nan somehow fit together—the way men sometimes treat women, the aggression that we grow up with, the way some men have the anger wire crossed with the love wire. So I combined Nan with Robin and made the situation similar to the way it happened, but in the story the mother leaves to visit a boyfriend, not to have an ear operation.

The opening of my first attempt began this way:

> The Big Ear, nearly as large as Peter, and brightly colored, stands out wherever he takes it, but no one really knows what it is, unless they ask. Peter practices withering looks on the people who ask, especially if they're kids. With the seriousness of purpose and steadiness of a Civil War photographer, he stands beside his Big Ear on its black tripod. He pretends to make fine calibrations on the plastic orange cone, bending into it and tapping it with a finger. Most people never get close enough to bother him with questions. That is one of the wonderful things about The Big Ear; it is a powerful device. You can set it up almost as far away from people as you like, 500 yards, and it still picks up what they're doing. It can listen through windows. It can penetrate plaster walls.

Not a bad beginning, but the story went seriously astray with the kidnapping. I knew what I wanted to do, but I just couldn't do it.

Structure

As stated earlier, stories that come from memory can be too episodic. Instead of a chain of events with a clear cause/effect relationship, you might be tempted to string together a bunch of loosely connected episodes from your life and call it a story. The cause/effect relationship doesn't need to be obvious, but it needs to be there to some extent. Otherwise, it's not a story.

A story needs direction. So if you go from your watermelon party when you were ten to a time when you caught sixty blue gills in the lake to the time you kissed your cousin in your grandma's tool shed, you might have "Scenes From a Happy Childhood," but you don't have a story. In stories based on real life, difficult distinctions must be made between what is necessary and what is merely an interesting but extraneous side note.

If your story seems too episodic, consider its structure. See how it all fits. List the scenes and what happens in them and see whether they're connected. Try structuring the story in a different way. Be flexible. Write five different titles. Write five different beginnings. Write five different outlines. Write five different outcomes. Loosen up and don't berate yourself if it doesn't work the first time.

The kidnapping in my Big Ear story, even though it had happened, didn't seem to belong. It almost seemed like another story. I was introducing another character late in the story, while before it had just been about Peter and the woman based on Nan.

This draft of the story ended in a silly fashion that I should be too embarrassed and intelligent to relate. But I'll relate it anyway. Remember the cigarette loads I mentioned earlier? They play a contrived role in this version.

> They tell him to go up the path, to stay in view. They've pulled off the road by a demolished building. It's only a pile of bricks and rusting furniture. Large spools of thread—red, white and yellow—stick out among the bricks. Peter walks to the other side of the heap. He can make out Sandy and Charlie's heads, but not their bodies. There's a long shack made of faded boards, one wall torn out, and inside are more spools of thread, the signs of a campfire, and broken school desks. He could run, he thinks. If their voices rise or if they're silent, he'll run. If they disappear from view, he'll run. He can run along the road or through the woods, though he knows this gangly man, who looks like a long distance runner, might easily overtake him, despite his smoking.
>
> He hears their voices, but can make no sense of them. He wishes he had his Big Ear. But the pain comes

through clearly, even if the words make no sense. Was that all he needed to understand, the pain they caused? That it was private, theirs alone, and he could never enter it? The clearest sound is the rustling of dry leaves, as sharp as breaking glass. The in-suck of breath from the lit cigarette.

He hears a pop and then Sandy says, "Oh God," and both their heads disappear behind the rubble of the broken building.

Peter runs toward the sound rather than away. He races around the bricks and spools of yarn and stops.

Charlie seems stunned. He stands there with the exploded cigarette in his mouth, and then he gets a reflective look and begins to cry. Sandy stands there with that same reflective look, and her shoulders begin to buckle, and she buries her face in her hands.

Peter wonders what he should do. He had hoped the exploding cigarette would divert Charlie's attention and give Sandy the advantage. But neither she nor Charlie seem to want the advantage now.

"I could never hurt you," he says.

"I know," she says, trying to quiet him.

Peter takes a step back. I've just been kidnapped, he wants to scream, but he's silent, trying his best to understand, though he knows now it's impossible to understand completely.

Then Sandy notices Peter. "You little fool," she yells at him.

He doesn't understand the rest of what she yells.

But I thought you were afraid, he's thinking, unsure of what could have gone wrong.

When his mother returns from Atlanta, he won't ask her about Guido. He doesn't want to know. And if she asks him about his week, he'll just say it was fine, and change the subject, and talk about what he wants for Christmas, a new fishing pole.

Peter stands there, blinking his eyes at Sandy, like it's some lost code between them.

She takes a step toward him, and Peter turns and runs.

I knew this wasn't very good about two seconds after I wrote it. There are some good details, but the action seems contrived and the dialogue seems melodramatic. Still, it's better to finish a draft of something terrible than to give up.

Changing Point of View

I decided to try a new approach. I thought maybe I was sticking too close to actual events, so I thought, *What if I tell it from a different point of view, say, a young girl's instead of a boy's. And what if I change the mother into a father. Maybe he's teaching at this all-girls' school and is having an affair with one of the students! Yeah, sure.* I also remembered something else from my childhood, a neighbor kid from when we lived in Athens, Ohio. His name was Bobby Bradley Biddle. I'm telling you his full name because that's how he always referred to himself. He had a strong country accent, and no matter how many times he spoke to you, he'd always introduce himself: "Hah, my name is Bobby Bradley Biddle." Bobby was a very gullible kid. No matter what you told him, he believed it. Of course, being the fledgling writer that I was, I tended to tell him a lot.

Then I remembered something else, this time from Columbia: these two girls I used to play with and their missionary father and mother. What if I combined Bobby Bradley Biddle with them and made his mother the student the narrator's father fools around with? My main problem here was that I didn't know my characters well enough. I had a situation in mind (boy with listening device, not understanding adult goings-on), but I didn't know who any of the characters were besides this boy. He was me when I was twelve—though not completely. He was me exaggerated. But with the other characters I was floundering. Here's what I came up with this time:

> "Hi, Justine, my name is Bobby Bradley Biddle," Bobby said to me when I opened the door. He had a strong accent, so what he said to me actually sounded like, "Hah, Justine, mah nayem's Bobay Bradlay Beetle."
>
> He'd only been to my house a million times, but this was a strong habit with Bobby Bradley Biddle, announcing his full name wherever he went, like he was sure

people would forget him the moment he left their sight.

Bobby smiled shyly at me and said, "Remember me?"

"Elvis Presley?" I asked.

"Nope," he said.

"Duke Ellington?"

"Nope," he said and laughed. "I don't even know any Duke Ellingtone."

"Then you're going to have to leave. I don't know you."

"Sure you do," he said, but he didn't laugh this time. He looked ultra-serious. "Sure you know me," he said. "I'm Bobby Bradley Biddle."

"What was that middle name?"

"Bobby."

"Oh, now I remember you," I said, and let him in.

Fine, but what happened to the Big Ear? I decided to scrap this version as well. Okay, back to the kidnapping. Maybe if I started the story with the kidnapping and changed the point of view again it would work. Worth a try, anyway.

In the car, Joe asks Anthony if he's kidnapping them. Nora, still dressed in her heavy tae kwon do *gi*, tied with a yellow belt, stares out the window, which is wide open. Anthony didn't even give her a chance to change at the house. "No one's kidnapped anyone," Anthony says softly. "I just don't want to let you go." Anthony seems, to Joe, like a nice guy, not like someone who wants to or could harm anyone. He told Joe before he worked with mentally challenged children. He said it was sometimes rewarding, sometimes heartbreaking.

I guess I can't write good kidnappings. My heart just wasn't in it. To me, it didn't ring true at all, which brings up an interesting point: I *was* actually kidnapped at that age (albeit briefly), but it seemed less "true" than many of the events I imagined for the story. When I say it doesn't ring true, I mean that it doesn't ring true to me. Perhaps if I showed it to someone else, he might say it looks perfectly fine. In some ways, we're not talking about the authenticity of the event; it might seem like a perfectly authentic kidnapping. But the scene didn't ring true to the story I wanted to write, even if I wasn't completely sure what that story was. It didn't fit. It seemed to take the story away from the central character too much. It worked against the focus of the story, which was Peter. So I had to take it out.

Getting Distance

The distance I'm talking about means setting aside your draft for a while, for however long it takes so you can see it with a clear perspective and a cool eye. Don't rush your revisions. If your story takes two or three years to gel, allow yourself that time.

I gave up on the story for a year or two. That might have been the best thing I could have done. It gave me time to get distance. I was too close to the material, even though it was by this time far removed from my real-life experiences.

Finally, when I was ready I went back to Justine and Bobby Bradley Biddle. This time, I decided to get back to the Big Ear and make sure it was an integral part of the story.

> Now I'm in my activist phase, but I used to be big on party gags. "By the time you grow up, Justine," Mom says, "you're going to break the Guinness world record for most phases." She's wrong. Petition drives, environmental issues, the nuclear thing—that kind of stuff is what I'm making my life's work. But back when I lived with my dad half the year, I clowned around all the time. It started with this catalogue I found an ad for in the back of a comic book. The ad showed a little cartoon guy with a big head and electrocuted hair poking his finger into a light socket. A bunch of other cartoon guys who looked just like him surrounded the little guy, and they were bent over double, pointing their fingers at him. "HA HA HA!" was written in bold black letters all around the ad, and in smaller letters were the words, "Thousands of gags for incredibly low prices!"
>
> What I really wanted from the catalogue was the Big Ear, an electronic listening device, so that I could go out

to Stephen's Lake and listen to all the couples making out on their blankets.

My dad didn't like teaching at Stephens and used to complain about its reputation as a finishing school for Southern belles, where women majored in subjects like equestrian science. Once, when he was getting ready to leave for school, he gathered up his scattered things around the house by galloping like a horse.

"Where are my keys?" he shouted. "Come on noble steed or we'll be late for class." He clucked his tongue and shook the reins.

I pointed to the Big Ear and said, "Do you think you could afford this for my birthday?"

My Dad bent down and said, "We'll see, Justine."

He turned his attention away from me and started scanning the kitchen counter, then sifted through the tons of paper, rubbing his hands across the surface like a miner sifting for gold in a stream. "I can't leave without my keys," he said finally. "Did you see them?"

"You're always losing your keys," I said. "I should get you an electronic keyfinder. They have one in the catalogue. When you lose your keys you have a little beeper that finds it for you."

Not a bad voice, but this one wasn't right either, so I went back to the kidnapping. Finally, I got so sick of going back and forth that I looked at my story with a cold eye and thought, *How many stories am I telling?* By my count, about half a dozen.

Telling One Story Well

What I needed to do, I finally figured out, was to drop all the extra memories and tell one story well, not six stories poorly. So, I dropped the kidnapping altogether. I went back to the male narrator. I dropped Bobby Bradley Biddle. I focused on the Big Ear and the main character's relationships to his mother and the character based on Nan. I began the story with the same beginning I'd started with, but this time I stayed focused. And, in the end, the story did everything I'd wanted it to do. My main character, Peter, basically listens to other people's pain. His mother is trapped in this going-nowhere, long-distance affair. The woman he was staying with, however, is somewhat stronger than Peter's mother. And, in the end, Peter comes to some understanding of what he's been listening to all along. The story is smaller, in some ways, in its conception than it was originally, but now it's more successful, I think. It doesn't end with a bang, but it ends more realistically. And I replaced the kidnapping with a remembered incident of being abandoned in Europe that a woman once told me when I was in college.

Most afternoons, Peter sets up his Big Ear in the front yard of his house and points the device down the road. Peter doesn't always know what he wants to listen for. Sometimes it reassures him when he doesn't hear anything.

Sandy spends half her days out back, practicing her tae kwan do, the house between them.

At night they sit up in his mother's room, where Sandy is sleeping. They sit crosslegged on the bed, and she sings for him, ancient folk songs about lonesome murderers. For someone who's so small, her voice is deep and rich, and suited to songs of backwood hollows and the hangings of innocent and guilty men. He never asked Sandy to sing, and she didn't really offer. It just happened the first night after dinner. After that first night, they were friends. She doesn't only sing, but she talks to him, too. She tells him things about her life that no stranger has ever told him. Not even his mother. She tells him about a trip last year to Europe with a man named Phil, and how they argued, and how he left her in the middle of this bridge with no money and no way to get home.

"What did you do?"

"I managed."

"How could he do that?" Peter asks. He imagines a giant white bridge with pillars topped by lions' heads, Sandy standing in the middle of the deserted bridge, and a bent figure in a trenchcoat hurrying away.

Peter remembers the day his father left them. They were in the kitchen. Peter's mother said he was threatened by women, and his father laughed.

"You know it goes both ways," he said.

"Yes it does," she answered calmly. "I'm not denying that. It's natural to feel threatened. Why shouldn't we feel threatened? That's the only thing we're experts at, inspiring fear and weathering it."

"I'm not afraid of you," he'd said.

"You're not listening," she said calmly, her arms folded, but Peter could see she was trembling.

Peter takes out a pack of Wrigley's gum from his pocket, but if you look closely at the wrapping, you notice that it doesn't really say Wrigley's but Wriggles. So Peter always feels justified when he offers people this gum. If they're paying attention they'll notice the fake name and won't fall for the trick, a mouse trap that snaps on your finger when you pull the stick of gum from the pack.

He thinks of the last person he offered the gum to, a girl named Susan Macnamara. Susan wanted to go steady with him a few months back, and he agreed, but he didn't know what he was getting into. One day, she led him down to a gully near her house, to a hollowed-out log where she said she used to sit and think. She told him she had a surprise for him and then kissed him.

"Ow," Peter said.

Susan pulled back. "Ow? Why'd you say ow?"

"I don't know," he said, feeling ashamed. "I thought you were going to do something to me."

"Peter Costello. You're not supposed to say 'ow' when a woman kisses you."

"Okay," he said and closed his eyes and puckered his lips. But she didn't feel like kissing him now. That's when he offered her the gum.

"Phil sounds mean," Peter tells Sandy.

Sandy looks up at the ceiling and says, "I never thought of Phil as mean when I was with him. He didn't do anything outwardly cruel. But it was inside of him all the time. To this day, he probably gets a kick out of it, thinks it proved something that he was able to abandon me like that. If I ever see him again . . . All my life I've been involved with murderers. Part of the attraction of the relationship was the pain, but I really think that's the last time I'm going to let that happen. That's why I'm taking tae kwan do, not so much for the self-defense, but for the confidence. I *was* taking judo. Judo teaches you to use the attacker's own force against him, but you know what? It doesn't work. We've been going that route much too long. I'm never going to put myself in that position again. You know that Billie Holliday song, 'God Bless the Child That's Got Its Own'?"

Peter shakes his head no, entranced.

"Do you want to hear it?" She starts to sing, but she stops and looks at him seriously. "You're not going to be that way, are you? You wouldn't leave anyone stranded in the middle of a bridge."

"Not you," Peter answers.

She narrows her eyes and says, "Not anyone."

"Okay," Peter says.

"Promise?"

Peter nods.

Sandy bends over and kisses Peter's forehead, strands of her hair tickling his face. He doesn't understand how someone could hate her as much as Phil must have. He imagines himself and Sandy together when he's thirty, watching TV, picking up nonsense on the Big Ear.

"I like this," Sandy says.

"Me too."

"Men should stay twelve, don't you think?"

"Indubitably," Peter says.

"Come to think of it," she says, but doesn't finish the thought. "Oh, you have gum?" she says, reaching for it.

"It's my last piece," he says. "I'm saving it." Peter puts the gum back in his pocket. He knows how selfish that sounds. He'd like Sandy to read his mind, to know she doesn't really want this fake gum. She smiles and touches his leg and says, miraculously, "That's fine. I don't need it."

Peter hears the telephone ringing. It's his mother. He knows her ring, and he knows what she's going to say before she says it, that things with Antoine didn't work out, that she misses Guido, that she's returning home early. Peter looks at Sandy and she looks at him, and for some reason, they both burst out laughing. He wishes that it could always be like this, that he could relay and receive telepathic messages, speak different languages, that distance didn't matter, that every nerve in his body was attuned to the slightest sounds.

By the way, a line or two that Sandy says is something that a friend told me one day during the time I was working on the story. "All my life I've been involved with murderers. Part of the attraction of the relationship was the pain." When my friend told me this, I nodded my head sympathetically, then I asked him if I could use it. Perhaps, now that I've alerted you to the theme running throughout the story — of pain in relationships — this passage, too, might seem like so much scaffolding. But if you come across it naturally in the course of Sandy's dialogue (and haven't read my previous drafts), I don't think it will stick out too much.

Sharpening the Knife

There's no set way to go about revising. It's a matter of trial and error. With material from real life, people have the natural tendency to include the kitchen sink and see everything they've written as crucial to the story simply because "it really happened." To you, the writer, the connection between remembered events is implicit: They're connected because they happened to you. But that's not the way it will work for everyone else reading the story. It's not important to anyone else simply because it happened to you. If you write fiction, you must learn to be brutal with your own work — and your life. Many times, other people to whom you show your work either aren't invested enough in what you write to offer you truly helpful suggestions, or else they're simply at a loss as to what you can do to improve the story. So you must rely on your own instincts eventually and become your own strongest critic.

Exercises

1. Count the number of words in a story you've written from real life, perhaps one you're having trouble focusing. Now cut the story in half. Cut it in half again. What you're left with will be the essentials of the story, and you'll be able to see it more clearly.

2. If your story lacks focus, if it seems to ramble from one episode to another based on your life, change the point of view. Make it not your life.

3. Try writing a scene based on your life in a different genre. Turn it into a science fiction piece. Turn it into a thriller, a horror story, a comedy.

4. Write a two-page description of the area you now live in — your city, town or neighborhood — as if you plan to use this area as the setting for a piece of fiction. Try to evoke a vivid sense of what this place is like today. Next, research the area at the local library, at the area historical society, or by interviewing long-time residents of the place. Then rewrite your description, enriching it with the facts, details and anecdotes acquired through your research.

5. Go to the microfilm section of your library and find a newspaper from fifty years ago. Examine it from front to back and use this paper as a guide for setting a scene on this exact day fifty years ago. Ignore most of the headlines. Look at the small stories and the ads. Use the advertisements to dress your characters. Use the classifieds or the movie section or the funnies to give them something to talk about.

CHAPTER EIGHT

Legal and Ethical Concerns

Recently, I was approached by a woman who had a story that "needs to be told." Actually, it wasn't her story, but the story of a friend of hers. The woman whose story it was didn't know that the other woman was planning to tell her story and perhaps would be angry if she knew about it. In other words, the woman's story *didn't* need to be told. Frankly, no story *needs* to be told. A story is not a concrete thing—not something you can bring home like a baby from the hospital, feed it, nurture it and then send it out into the world where it can be told. A story depends on the teller. The woman "whose story needs to be told" doesn't know that her story needs to be told, perhaps doesn't care except that it might embarrass her if people she knew connected her with the story. For her, it's not a story. It's a life.

I asked the woman why the other woman's story needs to be told, and she answered, "Because she's going to die soon." That's not really a reason for telling a story, since we're all going to die soon, relatively speaking. "It's about teen violence," she went on, "and it's important because there's so much of it going on today." I asked her if it needed to be written as fiction, or if it was better suited for nonfiction. She knew nothing at all about fiction, she said, but she wanted to write it as fiction because she wanted to disguise it so the woman whose story "needs to be told" wouldn't be able to "prove anything."

All of this is tricky territory, but a lot of it depends on one's personal sense of ethics. On the one hand, you can't copyright an anecdote told at a party, a secret told in confidence or any other life experience. But you should be aware of other people's feelings and realize that what you write might inadvertently hurt someone in your family or ruin a friendship.

The word "inadvertently" is important here because some people are thin-skinned and don't understand what fiction is. Your mother, perhaps, sees herself in every story you write. You have a story in which the mother slaps her child. "I never slapped you!" your mother screams when she reads the story. "It's not about you," you say. "It's fiction." A little later, she shouts, "I didn't know you smoked pot in high school!" "I didn't, Mom. It's a story." Sometimes, when you *have* written pretty directly about your friends or relatives, they don't recognize themselves at all. That's really not so amazing. You might see your Aunt Imelda as avaricious and petty, but she sees herself as the most generous-spirited soul alive. And who's to say who's right? Maybe you're the avaricious and petty one, and you're just projecting your shortcomings onto Aunt Imelda. In any case, Aunt Imelda reads your story and thinks it's precious. She's just proud you've written a story and she tells you she's going to brag to her friends about you. Now, don't you feel guilty?

DISCLAIMERS

Here's a secret: Those disclaimers in the front of novels that read, "Any resemblance to persons, living or dead, is purely coincidental," don't mean a thing. In a legal sense, disclaimers do not provide protection from or defense against lawsuits. If someone feels your characterization is not in the least coincidental and decides to sue you for libel or invasion of privacy, pointing to your disclaimer won't help. In a creative sense, and let's be honest, the resemblance is not coincidental at all. Every writer uses real people as the basis for fictional characters. There's even an encyclopedia of real people who were the models for fictional creations. The book is called *The Originals: An A-Z of Fiction's Real-Life Characters*, by William Amos (Little, Brown). For instance, look under "M" and you'll discover that Miss Marple, at least in part, was based on Agatha Christie's grandmother. Look under "T" and you'll discover that Elliott Templeton in W. Somerset Maugham's *The Razor's Edge* is based on Sir Henry ("Chips") Channon who, the son of a Chicago businessman, wanted to "become more English than the English."

Characters rarely come from nowhere, though they aren't always based on one person. As I've mentioned previously, characters most often are composites of several people we've met in our lives. Maybe you met these people by chance, but that's about as coincidental as it gets. Even Maugham's friend Chips was a composite. Apparently, Chips *wanted* to be portrayed by Maugham as Templeton, but Maugham delivered more than Chips bargained for. Chips explained, "[H]e had split me into three characters, and then written a book about all three." I suppose that makes Chips not a composite but the opposite, a real person split into three characters. Perhaps a prismite?

Still, disclaimers are part of the business and on occasion have risen to an art form. Frederick Exley has one of the best in his book, *Fan's Notes*:

> Though the events in this book bear similarity to those of that long malaise, my life, many of the characters and happenings are creations solely of the imagination. In such cases, I, of course, disclaim any responsibility for their resemblance to real people or events, which would be coincidental. The character "Patience," for example, who is herein depicted as "my wife," is a fictionalized character bearing no similarity to anyone living or dead. In creating such characters, I have drawn freely from the imagination and adhered only loosely to the pattern of my past life. To this extent, and for this reason, I ask to be judged as a writer of fantasy.

Hemingway, in *To Have and Have Not*, also uses the disclaimer to good effect:

> In view of a recent tendency to identify characters in fiction with real people, it seems proper to state that there are no real people in this volume: both the characters and their names are fictitious.

Hemingway was being coy. A number of his characters were based on real people, including very unflattering portraits of John Dos Passos and his wife, Katy Smith Dos Passos—so unflattering, in fact, that Arnold Gingrich, publisher of *Esquire*, urged Hemingway to take out the potentially libelous passages from the book. Gingrich claimed that the characterizations were so transparent and vicious as to invite legal action.

In the passages, Hemingway characterizes Dos Passos as a hypocrite who pretends to be "incorruptible" and borrows from his friends on the basis of his sterling reputation, with no intention of paying them back. It's "like a trust fund," one Hemingway character says to another. Katy Dos Passos comes off even worse. She's characterized as a kleptomaniac who "likes to steal as much as a monkey does."

According to Robert E. Fleming in *The Journal of Modern Literature*, Hemingway took Gingrich's advice and expunged the offending paragraphs from the manuscript. He even changed the description of the character based on Dos Passos, making him a handsome man when, in fact, Dos Passos was balding, skinny and wore thick glasses that hardly made him the Hemingway model of male perfection. (Fleming notes that it's possible Hemingway simply removed the paragraphs for artistic reasons rather than worries of a libel suit. Hemingway tended to write vicious attacks on former friends, attacks he never intended to publish, such as *The Autobiography of Alice B. Hemingway*, in which he attacks Gertrude Stein.) In any case, what prompted this attack of vitriol on Hemingway's part? Poor fishing off Cuba? Bad hair day? No, apparently Hemingway was one of those unfortunates who had loaned Dos Passos money, $1,000 in 1933 when Dos Passos was convalescing from rheumatic fever. Dos Passos did have a reputation of incorruptibility, someone who wouldn't follow the latest trends, who attacked the moneyed interests of J.P. Morgan and William Randolph Hearst and who, according to Hemingway, "wouldn't change a comma if you put him on the rack. You could break him on the wheel but the word *merde* stays in, you know." Fleming claims that by attacking Dos Passos' integrity, Hemingway supposed he was slamming his former friend where "it would hurt most."

WRITING WELL IS THE BEST REVENGE

Hemingway isn't the only writer who gets revenge on the real world in a fictional one. This is perhaps not the noblest of reasons for writing about someone else, but almost every writer tries it at one time or another. Nora Ephron got ex-husband Carl Bernstein good in *Heartburn* (Knopf). Perhaps revenge wasn't her motive, but the portrait of him is certainly scathing, and it definitely steamed him up. This is perhaps the most common type of revenge, casting a former spouse in a villainous role, and publishers cringe at the thought of such portraits and the attendant lawsuits that sometimes follow. Even if your motive isn't revenge, it still might not be the wisest idea to write about a former lover or spouse in a disparaging way, especially someone who might not hold you in the highest regard, either.

Terry McMillan found this out when she based a character on her former boyfriend in her novel *Disappearing Acts* (Viking). In the novel, she gave him the same occupation, the same education, and he even ate the same breakfast cereal. But the man in the novel also abuses alcohol and drugs and beats his girlfriend. That characterization upset Leonard Welch, her ex-boyfriend, and he sued for nearly $5 million. The judge dismissed the case. According to *The Wall Street Journal*, the judge, in his decision, wrote, "[A] reasonable reader couldn't possibly attribute the defamatory aspects of the character [Franklin Swift] to Mr. Welch, even though the character seems to be modeled on Mr. Welch. . . . But the man in the novel is a lazy, emotionally disturbed alcoholic who uses drugs and sometimes beats his girlfriend," said Judge Spodek, while "Leonard Welch is none of these things."

Another apparent revenge case was that of *Springer v. Viking Press* in 1983. Lisa Springer, a college girlfriend of Robert Tine, claimed the novelist added a character, Lisa Blake, to his novel in revenge for the breakup of their relationship. Lisa Blake was exactly like Springer in her physical description, where she lived, her hobbies, her vacations, even her jewelry. The only difference was that Lisa Blake was characterized as a high-priced prostitute.

Perhaps a little tacky and juvenile on Tine's part, but the courts found, as in the McMillan case, that no reasonable person who knew Springer would believe that she was indeed a prostitute.

Despite that the novelists won in these cases, it's better to avoid the mess by doing something more aggravating to your exes than dumping them in your fiction. How about signing them up for all those aircraft technician schools you find on match book covers?

Now *there's* a more mature revenge.

Of course, I'm not above a little revenge. I put the last names of some people I didn't like on tombstones in *The Last Studebaker*. There's nothing defamatory in that, except they're dead. I also got mild revenge in the same novel on a restaurant that wanted to serve my wife fish and chips without french fries. The absurd conversation that followed was lifted nearly verbatim from the actual occurrence, including the manager's contention that, "We don't mean fish *and* chips. We mean fish cut *into* chips." Yes, someone literally said that. So, while I'm not in favor of getting revenge on exes in print, I'm all for going after bad restaurants and banks and anything else that contributes to the myriad frustrations of contemporary life. Even so, it would be wise to change the name or locale of the offending institution.

SO SUE ME!

It might seem as if you can't write about anyone without the fear of being sued for libel, but that's not true. McMillan said, quite rightly, after the judge's decision in her case, "Every writer takes things from his or her own life, but you alter them. I hope this decision will reassure other authors, too, to just exhale and get on with what we do." This was considered a major victory for authors and publishers, primarily because it dealt with one of the main characters in the book, not a minor one as in past cases.

There's a great catch-22 at work here for the fiction writer. Obviously, the suit is without merit, goes the logic of the decision in the McMillan case, because the characterization is so blatantly false. On the other hand, if Welch *were* a drug addict and girlfriend beater, the accusations would be true, and therefore the suit would likewise be without merit, since true accusations are not defamatory.

You can be sued for almost anything, though that doesn't mean the lawsuit will stand up in court. If your mother sues you because your character who slaps her children is loosely based on her, your lawyer counters by saying, "That's why it's called fiction. Everyone who knows you knows you'd never slap your children." And then your mother drops her lawsuit because she is, after all, your mom.

According to an article in *The New York Times Magazine* by Judge Irving R. Kaufman, things can and have gone the other way, using just the *opposite* logic of the above catch-22. The plaintiff shows the similarities between himself and the character in a novel or a short story, and then shows any deviation as evidence that the portrayal is false.

In 1979, Gwen Davis wrote a novel based on a nude encounter group in California. She had signed an agreement with the leader of those sessions, psychologist Paul Bindrim, that she would not write about the group, and she didn't. She fictionalized it. In her book, the head of the encounter group was described as a "fat Santa Claus type with long white hair, white sideburns, a cherubic rosy face and rosy forearms." Bindrim, however, was short-haired and clean-shaven.

Bindrim sued, claiming that she distorted the events of his group. Bindrim won, and his suit was upheld on appeal, the majority of the judges finding "overwhelming evidence that plaintiff and Herford [the name of the fictional character] were one." However, the lone dissenting judge noted in his opinion, "the fictitious Dr. Herford has none of the characteristics of plaintiff except that Dr. Herford practices nude encounter therapy." This decision set an absurd precedent. As Judge Kaufman points out in his *New York Times Magazine* article, it boils down to, "When you criticize my occupation, you libel me."

Bindrim collected $75,000 in damages from Davis and her publisher, Doubleday. Though that's not a vast sum by today's standards, it completely shocked the publishing industry. Partly as a result of that decision, publishers responded nobly and rallied round their authors with equal parts of self-protection and cowardice and made them sign contracts that basically said, "If you're sued, you're on your own." These "waivers of idemnification," as they are called, do not protect the publishers from lawsuits; they protect publishers from responsibility for lawsuits against the writer. Litigants, knowing where the big bucks can be made, almost always go after the publishers as well as the writers.

Today, most publishers have libel insurance and will go to bat for you, provided you disclose to them before publication anything that is potentially libelous. This is a key point. If you have a book accepted for publication, it's imperative to inform your publisher of any portrayals of real people in the work so the publisher's attorneys can review it against any potential libel claims. Disclose everything. If you have any doubts, err on the side of full disclosure. Ultimately, this will protect you.

In a similar case, Dr. Jane V. Anderson sued over the film version of Sylvia Plath's *The Bell Jar*. She and Plath had been patients at the same mental hospital, and she contended that she was the model for the character Joan Gilling, a suicidal lesbian. In court, her side argued that Anderson had never, in fact, made sexual advances toward Plath. "I also never made any suicide attempts or had scars on my breast. And certainly I never hung myself." That last statement seems a given. But if she *had* hanged herself, just imagine how much more potent her testimony would have been. The defense argued exactly the same thing. You're alive. You're here in court. Therefore, the character is fictitious.

This case was resolved in an out-of-court settlement. Who knows who would have won or what precedent it might have set, but it's understandable that both sides settled. The costs of such actions are so exorbitant that no one wins in the end.

Perhaps the most ludicrous literary libel case was the 1982 case of the former Miss Wyoming who sued a short story writer for a story that appeared in *Penthouse*. In this case, a fictional Miss Wyoming was characterized as performing all kinds of farcical sexual activities. The description of this Miss Wyoming was very stereotypical, something like blonde hair and blue eyes and she was a baton twirler. By coincidence, the real Miss Wyoming fit the story writer's portrait, and she sued. She won, too — $28 million! But the case was overturned by a federal appeals court, ruling that the sexual escapades were so bizarre that no one would believe a real person (not even from Wyoming) could perform them.

Again, that catch-22.

Now that I've thoroughly scared you, let me give you cause for cheer. It's rare for fiction writers to be sued, and when they are, the courts rarely award damages. Furthermore, most courts have not followed the precedent of the Gwen Davis case but follow the model of Terry McMillan's case. And McMillan's case is a much more recent precedent than the Davis case. Still, the costs of defending oneself against a libel action can be expensive, as well as emotionally disruptive, so it's not a good idea to take too cavalier an attitude toward such concerns.

The Associated Press Stylebook and Libel Manual defines libel as "injury to reputation." So, what then is libel in fiction? According to Judge Kaufman, certain conditions must be present: "The reference must clearly be 'of and concerning' the plaintiff. It must not be mere opinion." In other words, just because you have a character refer to George Will as a neo-Fascist pedant who's got his head up his duffel bag does not give him the right to sue. Last, the offending work "must be made with actual malice." Malice, in its legal sense, means that you know something is false but publish it anyway with "reckless disregard," according to the A.P. manual.

However, private citizens, as opposed to public figures, need not prove malice in court. They must simply prove negligence, meaning that the writer did not take the necessary care in proving the veracity of information before stating it as fact. As a general rule, the more public the figure, the greater the burden of proof necessary to win a libel case. This rule is based, of course, on freedom of speech. The more public the information, the greater its protection by the First Amendment. So George Will needs to amass stronger evidence of your intentions than does your ex-boss, who claims you libeled him in your latest novel.

So while we all use real people as models, we must be somewhat careful. That a characterization of someone real appears in a work of fiction does not automatically protect it from libel concerns. Moreover, the legal precedents are somewhat hazy and contradictory. Although, as mentioned earlier, most lawsuits against fiction writers are eventually dismissed, the legal costs of mounting a defense are prohibitive, so it's much better to do everything you can to avoid being sued in the first place.

Your best defense is written consent from the person you have fictionalized. Here's a list of other points to consider:

- Is your character an easily recognizable real individual?

- Have you written an unflattering portrait?

- Do you seek revenge on this person?

- Are the transformations of the character simply superficial ones?

- Have you neglected to tell your publisher or editor about any potentially libelous material?

If your answer is yes to any of these questions, you must go back and transform your material. To be safe, transform your characters as much as possible. Change the gender or locale. Use composites. Better to err on the side of conservatism than to be sued later.

For journalists, the only absolute defense against a libel suit is that the facts stated must be *provably* true. For fiction writers, there are no unconditional defenses. But for a characterization to be libelous, it must be *clearly* of and concerning the plaintiff. That's the opposite of the journalist's defense. Your defense is that it's clearly *not* true, that it's fiction.

REAL NAMES

A lot of writers have made the mistake of using someone's real name in a story or a novel. Some even do it on purpose. In the seventies, John Irving was a visiting writer at the Iowa Writers' Workshop and had a student named Jenny Fields. The story goes that Irving wanted to use her name in his new book, *The World According to Garp*. Apparently, Fields was not pleased with this, and she went to one of the permanent faculty members to complain. "There's nothing you can do about it," he told her. Names are fair game, as long as you do not use the person, too.

If Jenny Fields could prove that Irving's character was based on her and the novel publicly disclosed facts about her private life, she could try to stop publication. If she could prove that her reputation was damaged by the characterization or, again, that private facts had been made public, she could sue. But since Irving used only her name, for a character with no other ties to her, she was left without legal recourse. Most suits involving the use of someone's name pertain to famous names that are used without permission to sell a product. If, for instance, you begin selling Michael Jordan candy bars without first asking Mr. Jordan, he can sue. Writers need to worry about name appropriation suits only when they use the person to whom the name belongs.

Madison Smartt Bell learned this lesson when he inadvertently used a real name as well as the real person in his fiction. Libel insurance was new when Bell's first novel, *The Washington Square Ensemble* (Viking Penguin), came out, so he and a lawyer went over the book as closely as possible. "I confessed tiny, tiny details," he says. "We were changing things like the names of bars. That night I went to Studio 54 — the only time in my life, because a friend took me. I go into the men's room and out walks this guy who I'd known on a job, wearing a white tuxedo. He's giving me this big smile. I hadn't seen him in about eighteen months, and he was in the book with a very hostile characterization under his own name. I'd forgotten that this guy was ever real. He was not a friend. And he turned into this jerky character in the novel. Immediately after this strange and discomfiting encounter, I had to go back to my publisher and say there'd been this little oversight. As it happened, the characterization was just a minor role in the first chapter. I ended up deleting it. It didn't appear in the finished book. Regardless, writers have a great ability to delude themselves."

That's true. Sometimes, as strange as this might sound, you almost forget the boundary between your imagination and real people. You forget that people who really exist weren't made up by you. I know that sounds awful and solipsistic, but it's the natural result of living in your own little world half the day. So, something like that can easily happen if you're not careful. It happened to Oscar Hijuelos in his Pulitzer Prize-winning novel, *The Mambo Kings Play Songs of Love* (Farrar, Straus and Giroux). He used the name "Glorious Gloria Parker and Her All-Girl Rumba Orchestra." I know exactly why he did it, though I've never spoken to Mr. Hijuelos. He used the name because it's great. Who could make up a band name like that? This is pure conjecture, but he probably didn't know her whereabouts, didn't even know if she was still among the living, or maybe, like Bell, forgot this was a real person.

Glorious Gloria Parker was all too real and all too unhappy when she saw her name and former band portrayed in Hijuelos' book, and she sued him for $15 million for defamation of character. I love the supposedly defamatory passages in the book. One reads that the Mambo King "made it with three of the musicians who played with Glorious Gloria Parker and Her All-Girl Rumba Orchestra, among them a Lithuanian trombone player named Gertie." In the other passage, Hijuelos shows "Gloria huddled at a table drinking daiquiris," and then saying to the Mambo King, "Come on ya big lug, why don't you kiss me?"

Glorious Gloria was not amused, claiming that she was now unable to find bookings as a result of being cast as a "character in that dirty book." She also claimed that she'd led an exemplary life and neither drank nor smoked. Obviously, this was not someone who would ask some big lug to kiss her.

The judge dismissed this case too, writing that, "It is difficult to believe that an average reader would consider either of the passages defamatory."

A lot of writers, including myself and most of my friends, occasionally use the names of their friends in their novels or stories. These cameo appearances are designed for the mutual amusement of the writer and her friend. These are always expendable, sometimes off-stage, characters. In *The Last Studebaker*, I made my friend Jurek Polanski the executor of an estate. David Shields often includes me in his novels as some off-stage editor or other pesky character.

Sometimes writers find names in the phone book. There's nothing wrong with that, and it's unlikely that you'll be sued. Let's say you see the name Travis Boovy. You don't know Travis Boovy. You've never met the gentleman. You just like the name. So you don't know what he's really like, and you certainly can't maliciously and consciously defame the man. If you name a character John Smith and you make him someone who stuffs hash browns in his ears, are all the John Smiths in the world going to sue you?

PUBLIC FIGURES

Some writers use public figures in their books. Public figures are those people who are in the limelight: famous actors, politicians, musicians. This also includes ordinary people who have been thrust into the public spotlight through some newsworthy event. Here, we also encounter our privacy laws. According to the A.P. Manual, "When a person becomes involved in a news event, voluntarily or involuntarily, he forfeits the right to privacy. Similarly, a person somehow involved in a matter of legitimate public interest, even if not a bona fide . . . news event, normally can be written about with safety. However, this is different from publication of a story . . . that dredges up the sordid details of a person's past and has no current newsworthiness." As an example, the guide mentions the case of a prostitute who was tried for murder, acquitted, later married and lived a happy life until a motion picture appeared that used her real name and was billed as based on a true story. This was found to violate her right to privacy.

Satire, of course, would be nearly nonexistent if we didn't have our First Amendment right to verbally draw and quarter our politicians and entertainers. This falls under the heading of fair comment, satire being a form of opinion. That doesn't mean it's impossible to be sued by a public figure, but as it is, they rarely sue *The National Enquirer*. Still, let's say you're sued by Liz Taylor or Michael Jackson because of the novel in which you portray Macaulay Culkin as their secret love child. Oh lucky day. Think of the publicity. Your book will probably be a bestseller. Plus you'll win the court case anyway. No sweat. Still, if you're squeamish, go ahead and change the name like Joyce Carol Oates did in her novel *Black Water* (Dutton). This book is unquestionably about Senator Ted Kennedy and the Chappaquiddick tragedy, but Oates changed the names and the time frame (probably for artistic reasons as much, if not more, as for reasons of legality). So Kennedy becomes The Senator and Mary Jo Kopechne becomes Kelly. There's no way one can read the book without thinking of Chappaquiddick, but it's not meant to be a literal account, simply a literary exploration.

On the other hand, consider *The Public Burning* (Viking), by Robert Coover. This absurd, farcical book is partly narrated by Richard Nixon and deals with the conviction and executions of Julius and Ethel Rosenberg. But in Coover's retelling of this chapter of American history, Nixon goes to prison to see Ethel Rosenberg, where he unexpectedly falls in love with her. They start making out in her cell, but they're interrupted and are unable to consummate their passion for one another. However, unbeknownst to Nixon, while his pants were off, Ethel scrawled the words, "I am a scam" in lipstick on his buttocks. Also, in Coover's telling, the Rosenbergs are executed in Times Square. In the middle of this public event, Nixon gets up on stage and his pants fall down, revealing to the assembled multitude the words Ethel wrote on his rear end. In the midst of the uproar that follows, Nixon is sodomized by the spirit of Uncle Sam!

Whew, loses something in the retelling, doesn't it? Nixon was none too happy about this novel, and his lawyers were nearly able to scuttle the book before it was published. In any case, they delayed the book's publication and undoubtedly made Coover's life uncomfortable.

There are no absolute protections for fiction writers writing about public figures. Knowing that you'll probably win a lawsuit brought on by a such a person will not necessarily make you sleep better at night, again because of the legal fees you'll incur defending your book, as well as the disruption to your peace of mind. If you can thinly disguise such a person without destroying the integrity of your work, so much the better. If you feel you must use the real person in your work, steel yourself for any possibility. As I've said, fiction writers are rarely sued, and when they are, the lawsuits are usually without firm legal grounding, as in the case against Oscar Hijuelos. So there's no sure indicator whether you will be sued for your published work. Much depends on who wants to take issue with it. Of course, controversy has rarely hurt a book, but it might hurt you personally. Again, the rule of thumb is to transform when possible and discuss any doubts with your publisher.

HISTORICAL ACCOUNTS

Plenty of historically based novels have been written — Don Delillo's novel *Libra* (Viking), for one, a fictional account of the Kennedy assassination in which he mixes fact and fiction freely, from the character of Lee Harvey Oswald to a fictional C.I.A. operative. *Schindler's List* by Thomas Keneally (Simon and Schuster) is another example, a novel and later a movie based on the life of a German industrialist who managed to save a number of Jews from the gas chambers. Of course, the main characteristic these books have in common is that most of the principals in the book are either dead or fictional.

That someone you write about is no longer living might not necessarily shield you from legal concerns, especially if the person is recently deceased. Consider his heirs who might be happy to sue you for defamation of character. A woman I know decided not long ago to write a nonfictional account of a highly publicized murder trial in North Carolina. She contacted the principals who were still alive as well as their relatives and was promptly threatened with a lawsuit. Perhaps the lawsuit would have been without merit, especially since this was an account of historical record, but it was enough to frighten her. The lawsuit's grounds would most likely have been the right to privacy, since the murder was no longer newsworthy.

So she decided to transform the account into a fictional murder mystery. This does not necessarily make her any safer, unless she transforms the characters as much as possible — changing the locale, using composites, etc. Sometimes the threat of a lawsuit is enough to make a writer give up a project.

If you are concerned that your story may be legally actionable in some way, contact an attorney. If you can't afford one, try Volunteer Lawyers for the Arts. This is a nationwide organization of lawyers who offer free or reduced-fee legal services to people in the creative arts on matters related to practicing art. To locate the branch nearest you, write:

> Volunteer Lawyers for the Arts
> Sixth Floor
> 1 East 53rd Street
> New York, NY 10022

Even if you've based your story on a historical account that happened a hundred years ago, some people might still attempt to intimidate you, as happened to Philip Gerard with his novel, *Cape Fear Rising*. This novel deals with an infamous incident in the town of Wilmington, North Carolina, where Gerard lives. In 1898, a group of powerful white businessmen staged a coup, driving out the Reconstruction town government and massacring some of the town's black residents. Gerard has opted to use real names in his book, prompting a great deal of controversy in Wilmington. There have been grumblings of suing him, though so far no one has figured out any grounds for such a lawsuit. Gerard has done what many writers do: He's made a number of people very uncomfortable. That, however, is not something a good writer necessarily shies away from. Sometimes it's the writer's job to make people uncomfortable, especially if they'd rather sweep under the rug a shameful period of their history. "When I started writing the book," Gerard says, "I told virtually no one, because I knew that if I received pressure when I was writing it, the novel would have gone unwritten."

This also harks back to the idea of the outsider writing about a place. Often, the outsider sees the place with much more clarity and insight than the insider.

MISTAKEN IDENTITIES

Sometimes there are freak coincidences. A former teacher of mine once wrote a novel about a woman whose brother-in-law and sister worked behind the scenes, unbeknownst to her, to cheat her out of an inheritance. She made this all up, but it turns out that's exactly what her brother-in-law and sister were trying to do in real life, and the two sisters haven't spoken to each other since. Sometimes, as mentioned earlier, when you get to the emotional core of things, you brush uncomfortably close to what really happened.

More often than not, people don't recognize themselves in your work. On this subject, Madison Smartt Bell says, "My experience has been in cases where I did base a character on a real person, I showed it to the person to make sure it wasn't a problem, and the person would say, 'I don't mind, but this is not me.' But frequently people recognize themselves where you had no intention, in characters that don't resemble them at all. One woman's been angry with me for years, thinking this novel I'd written was all about her, and there were not even any women characters in the novel!"

The same thing happened to Steve Yarbrough, although his case is perhaps a little atypical of most writers. His literary landscape is well-defined in that he almost exclusively writes stories set in and around Indianola, Mississippi, the town in which he grew up. "I did a few book signings in Mississippi right after my first book came out," says Yarbrough, "and I was uncomfortable around my hometown. People had bought the book and read it, people who'd never read a work of fiction in their lives, and they were just reading it to see if they could find somebody they knew. One of my high school teachers called me up about two weeks ago. I hadn't talked to her in years and she told me she had read my first book, and she wanted me to confirm that this person was based on so-and-so and that person was based on somebody else. Very often her evidence would be something really preposterous like, "Well, I know that's so-and-so because you said he's more than six feet tall and his name starts with W.' When you're writing about a town of nine thousand like I am, it makes people want to make really huge assumptions."

It is doubtful that, in most cases, such mistaken or assumed identities are legally actionable. An outraged neighbor in your hometown would need to prove that a character is a thinly disguised version of her and that she has suffered damages as a result of your characterization. She must also prove that you have publicly disclosed private facts. "Private" is a key word here. You may write of a town figure who regularly gets drunk at the corner bar and starts fights — because he does this in a public place and his behavior is known to the public. But if this thinly disguised character goes home and beats his wife — or, like Miss Wyoming, engages in bizarre sexual behavior — he could have a case. Miss Wyoming, after all, won hers.

BEGGING, BORROWING AND STEALING

Two writers whom I interviewed for this book told me cases of writing about friends or acquaintances, but they wouldn't let me tell you their names or give you the exact circumstances of the genesis of their stories. And for good reason. In one case, the writer had written a story based on a rather insane acquaintance of his, someone he suspected of being slightly dangerous, and however remote the chances were that this man would ever read this book, the writer did not want this guy to know he'd written a story about him. Another writer I spoke with recounted an anecdote in which her child had been bullied by another child in the presence of the other child's mother. She had wanted to scold the friend's child but hadn't, and the friend had simply ignored the incident. This sparked a story, and in this case the writer didn't want her name used because she was afraid her friend would somehow connect herself to the incident and be angry.

We're all a bit sheepish when it comes to talking about where we get our material. And a bit paranoid. The fact is, real life is the stuff of fiction, and real people are the stuff of life. You can't avoid writing about real people, nor should you be expected to. The problem is that fiction deals with moments of crisis and with secrets. It deals with exactly the types of things real people would rather not have known about them. So how do you get around ruining a friendship? First, I must stress that not everything you write about another person could conceivably upset the person you're writing about. Most often, people are flattered that you think there's something in their lives worth writing about, and that's as it should be.

But in answer to the question about perserving a friendship: I don't know.

Some writers, like Madison Smartt Bell, check with their friends before writing about them, but I'd bet he's the exception. Most writers just write and hope their friends or family won't mind. Some writers don't even care. Faulkner said a writer is "completely amoral in that he will rob, borrow, beg, or steal from anybody and everybody to get the work done."

While not all of us are as callous as Faulkner, fiction writers are not necessarily great humanitarians. Writers sometimes unfortunately feel that their ambition justifies nearly anything. There's nothing wrong with ambition. It's necessary to some extent. But writers do not necessarily give a hoot how you feel about their writing your life story or stealing your ideas. If you don't want something from your life written about, don't tell a writer. Otherwise, you're asking for it. And, as I said before, you can't copyright experience. If you tell a writer about the time you almost drowned and he thinks it's a great story, don't blame him. Blame yourself for blabbing it to him.

So I'm giving you fair warning. My sense of ethics and fair play shift from story to story, depending on how much I like the idea. Sometimes (most times), I'm ready to relinquish or radically change a story idea so as not to embarrass someone, even if I know no one will ever know it's based on her except for the person in question. Other times, I'm willing to give up a friendship over a story. In fact, I have. I'm not happy about it. I'm not sure the story was worth the friendship. Probably not. But at the time, I was just as selfish as that woman who claimed she had a story "that needs to be told."

It's hard to be a writer and not alienate someone along the way. On this subject Steve Yarbrough says, "I suspect that one friendship was ruined by a story in my first book. The friend was someone who used to call me a lot, but he stopped calling about a year after the book came out. He lived on the East Coast, but the story is set in Mississippi. Still, I have the feeling that he saw himself in the story, and that may have ruined the friendship, and to tell you the truth, I feel terrible about it. I thought that I'd altered enough of the facts of that character's life that he would never see himself in the story. I don't think anyone but this particular individual would ever have matched up the character with him."

David Huddle puts it very well in his book *The Writing Habit*, when he writes:

> I believe the writer must do whatever he can to avoid . . .
> trouble, to keep from hurting feelings, but I believe
> finally he cannot allow the opinions and feelings of others
> to stop or to interfere with his writing. Maybe this is the
> ultimate selfishness, to say that one's own work is more
> important than the feelings of family and friends. Auto-
> biographical writing will bring you to the point of having
> to make not just one but a number of hard choices be-
> tween the life and the work.

I wish I could tell you that if you're careful and a nice person, you'll never run the risk of hurting someone's feelings in your writing. But, of course, I can't. If people see themselves in characters you never intended to base on them, how can you predict how they'll react to the characters you *have* intentionally based on them? If you're meant to write, your desire to write will eventually overcome all other considerations, and you'll write, regardless of what anyone else might think. Says Yarbrough, "A lot of things you have to do in business and in many fields, things that are sound business practices, sometimes hurt people. So this is sort of the conflict of being a fiction writer. If you're going to shut out all your experiences and those of people you know, you won't be left with much to write about."

There are undoubtedly instances in which you should probably back off, but I'll leave that to your own sense of ethics. When I was in graduate school at Iowa, a friend told me of a terribly traumatic occurrence that had happened to her in the not-too-distant past. Unfortunately, she told several people in the workshop about this traumatic event, confiding in them, getting it off her chest. Most of the people she told were trustworthy. I, for one, never even *thought* of writing about it. Written as fiction, it probably would come out seamy and melodramatic, a chunk of indigestible six o'clock news. But one of our number, a man who was widely considered one of the worst writers in the workshop, thought it would make a marvel-ous story and told her he was going to write about it. She asked him not to, and reluctantly, he agreed he wouldn't. But he lied. So my friend went to the same man Jenny Fields had complained to. He told her pretty much the same thing: that there's nothing you can do about it, and you shouldn't worry because it probably won't be published anyway. Of course, the book was published, and much to the amazement of everyone in the workshop, the writer got the biggest advance for that book that any of us had ever seen. Our first lesson: Trash sells. This experience upset my friend, and I don't blame her, but I have mixed feelings. I think it was unethical of the writer to tell her that he wasn't writing the story based on her life when he, in fact, was. But I also think that no one outside the workshop ever knew this story was based on my friend. It caused her psychic damage, but you should know to whom you're telling your stories, who you can trust.

Writers generally respect each other's turf, like wary gang members. But you can't always count on that, either. Remember, writers with Faulkner's attitude (if not his talent) abound, and many of them tend to believe their self-appointed genius justifies any cruelty. At Iowa, we used to make little copyright marks in the air with our fingers when we told an anecdote. If someone steals from me, I remember what Barry Hannah once told me when he was my teacher at Iowa: If you have only one idea as a writer, you can't be much of one.

I always run into people who have good stories to tell, but they're afraid what will happen if their crazy aunt or dying mother or best friend reads the piece. I don't know why they tell *me* their stories. I might not steal from your life, but I think it's bad luck to talk about your work before you write it. Your subconscious won't differentiate between an oral or a written telling of the story, and if you tell it to me, you might just lose interest in the subject. Your desire to tell your story might slip away. Usually, I tell people to write their stories about their crazy aunts or insane friends and worry about it later. If your story means something to you, if it's important to you, write it, transform it as much as possible, and decide what to do with it later. Sometimes we feel too much guilt about these things. If you write the story sensitively, if you care about the subject matter, maybe you'll turn out something beautiful, a celebration and questioning of life in all its complexity, something that you and all your crazy friends can identify with.

Index